teach yourself

writing essays and
dissertations

teach yourself ®

writing essays and dissertations
hazel hutchison

For over 60 years, more than
50 million people have learnt over
750 subjects the **teach yourself**
way, with impressive results.

be where you want to be
with **teach yourself**

WANDSWORTH LIBRARY SERV

501201193

For UK order enquiries: please contact Bookpoint Ltd, 130 Milton Park, Abingdon, Oxon, OX14 4SB. Telephone: +44 (0) 1235 827720. Fax: +44 (0) 1235 400454. Lines are open 09.00–17.00, Monday to Saturday, with a 24-hour message answering service. Details about our titles and how to order are available at www.teachyourself.co.uk

For USA order enquiries: please contact McGraw-Hill Customer Services, PO Box 545, Blacklick, OH 43004-0545, USA. Telephone: 1-800-722-4726. Fax: 1-614-755-5645.

For Canada order enquiries: please contact McGraw-Hill Ryerson Ltd, 300 Water St, Whitby, Ontario, L1N 9B6, Canada. Telephone: 905 430 5000. Fax: 905 430 5020.

Long renowned as the authoritative source for self-guided learning – with more than 50 million copies sold worldwide – the **teach yourself** series includes over 500 titles in the fields of languages, crafts, hobbies, business, computing and education.

British Library Cataloguing in Publication Data: a catalogue record for this title is available from the British Library.

Library of Congress Catalog Card Number: on file.

First published in UK 2007 by Hodder Education, 338 Euston Road, London, NW1 3BH.

First published in US 2007 by The McGraw-Hill Companies, Inc.

This edition published 2007.

The **teach yourself** name is a registered trade mark of Hodder Headline.

Copyright © 2007 Hazel Hutchison

In UK: All rights reserved. Apart from any permitted use under UK copyright law, no part of this publication may be reproduced or transmitted in any form or by any means, electronic or mechanical, including photocopy, recording, or any information, storage and retrieval system, without permission in writing from the publisher or under licence from the Copyright Licensing Agency Limited. Further details of such licences (for reprographic reproduction) may be obtained from the Copyright Licensing Agency Limited, of Saffron House, 6–10 Kirby Street, London, EC1N 8TS.

In US: All rights reserved. Except as permitted under the United States Copyright Act of 1976, no part of this publication may be reproduced or distributed in any form or by any means, or stored in a database or retrieval system, without the prior written permission of the publisher.

Typeset by Transet Limited, Coventry, England.
Printed in Great Britain for Hodder Education, a division of Hodder Headline, an Hachette Livre UK Company, 338 Euston Road, London, NW1 3BH, by Cox & Wyman Ltd, Reading, Berkshire.

The publisher has used its best endeavours to ensure that the URLs for external websites referred to in this book are correct and active at the time of going to press. However, the publisher and the author have no responsibility for the websites and can make no guarantee that a site will remain live or that the content will remain relevant, decent or appropriate.

Hachette's policy is to use papers that are natural, renewable and recyclable products and made from wood grown in sustainable forests. The logging and manufacturing processes are expected to conform to the environmental regulations of the country of origin.

Impression number   10 9 8 7 6 5 4 3 2 1
Year   2012 2011 2010 2009 2008 2007

contents

acknowledgements

This book began as a set of photocopied handouts for my students at the University of Aberdeen. It quickly developed into a short booklet for English students, which found its way into many other departments of the university before I realized what had happened. Since then, a number of students and colleagues have contributed ideas, materials and enthusiasm, which helped me to rewrite and redesign the book into its present form. I am grateful to them all. In particular I would like to thank: Nuala Booth, Liz Curtis, David Duff, Jeannette King, Gert Ronberg and Tim Tricker, for comments and ideas early in the project; David Hutchison and Lorna Philip for permission to use original material; and Neil Curtis and Jonathan Pettitt for reading sections of the text. Thank you also to the Teach Yourself team at Hodder for support and advice.

dedication

This book is dedicated to Carrie and Jamie for when you are old enough to write your own essays and dissertations.

About this book

Writing is important. The ability to communicate clearly and effectively is one of the most useful skills you can learn. Whatever you study at school, college or university, and whatever career you choose, a command of language is a valuable asset. Learning to write well can add some extra polish and a few extra marks to your course work; it can also help to sharpen the way that you think. Good language skills are vital in the workplace, where many different kinds of jobs require the ability to write reports, letters or marketing copy, or to give talks or presentations.

This book will show you how to write well. It focuses on writing essays and dissertations as part of assessed work at college or university, and will also be helpful for projects in the final stages of study at school. It explains what markers are looking for in written work and how to achieve this. Tutors often reserve around 20 per cent of an essay mark for issues of presentation and expression, so improving in these areas can make a dramatic difference to your results. Good language skills will also help you create stronger arguments and present your ideas in the best light. Writing well is vital for success at all levels of study. Good writing is also important in many different areas of life, so the advice in this book will be of benefit to others with a wide range of jobs and interests.

Many people are daunted by concepts such as grammar, essay structure or referencing, especially if they prefer working in a subject with a strong practical or scientific element. If this applies to you, do not worry. Good writing isn't rocket science – not even if you are studying rocket science. Most common language problems are easy to fix, and the underlying principles of good writing are simple. Having said that, the process of learning to write well is never complete; there is always something else to correct or to try out. So, even if you are a confident writer, I hope that this book will give you things to think about and will help you to develop your own style and voice.

How to use this book

Every piece of writing, whether an academic essay, a newspaper article, a medical report or a book about writing essays, has a particular job to do, in a particular context, for a particular kind of reader. One of the hardest things about academic writing is working out exactly what sort of format you are supposed to follow and what tone of voice you are supposed to use. This can vary from subject to subject, sometimes even from project to project. However, the basic rules of good writing are the same across the board. You will produce good work when you:

1 Understand what sort of piece you are writing and who will read it.
2 Plan your structure carefully, so that your argument runs clearly.
3 Use language correctly and efficiently.
4 Use your sources effectively and reference them properly.

The four parts of this book are designed to improve your skills in each of these areas.

Part one: Where do I start? encourages you to think about the kind of work you are doing and what your marker will be looking for.

Part two: Building your answer gives advice on finding resources and on how to structure your work. It also looks at the tricky business of writing introductions and conclusions.

Part three: Using language tackles some of the most common problems in spelling and grammar, and looks at the kind of language which is appropriate for academic work.

Part four: Using sources explains how to choose the right material for your project and how to incorporate it into your writing. It shows how to avoid plagiarism and how to cite references in the standard styles.

You might need more advice in some of these areas than others. Different readers may want to use this book in different ways. You can start at the beginning and work right through. This will work best alongside your own preparation of a real essay or dissertation. The sections are in roughly the order in which you would put together a piece of written work, from understanding your project to tidying up your bibliography. If you decide to use the book this way, leave plenty of extra time. It will take much longer than writing an essay usually does, so do not start a couple of days before the deadline.

Alternatively, you can use this book as a handy reference guide to glitches and problems, looking up problem areas as they arise. There is an index at the back, so that you can find things quickly in an essay emergency, or when your marker complains about something which you do not understand. Throughout the book you will find **Ask yourself** sections, which will get you thinking about how you can apply what you are learning to your own work. You will also find **Top tip** sections, which give some handy hints on how to survive essay stress and avoid some common pitfalls. At the end of each chapter, you will find a **Quick fix** section. This gives an instant summary of the chapter for when you are really in a rush. At the end of each part, you will also find a **Try it out** section, with questions to think about and exercises to do when you have a little more time. Answers are given at the back of the book. At the end of the book, you will also find a **Taking it further** section which provides a list of suggested further reading. Many of these books and websites were helpful as I was writing this book and you may find them useful too.

What happens next?

You do not need to stop learning when you get to the end of this book. Look at some of the guides available in print and online about writing and study skills, and consider investing in a book specifically about referencing. Your school, college or university probably has some useful resources in these areas too. Have a look on your college website or ask at the library. Many institutions have members of staff dedicated to teaching study skills, and some of these offer one-to-one advice to students at all levels from freshers through to postgraduates. Find out what is on offer near you and take advantage of any available expertise. It will pay off. Talk to your tutors about your written work and ask them to spend some time in class discussing upcoming assessments. If you do not feel you are getting helpful feedback on your work, make an appointment to see your tutor to discuss it. Most staff are delighted to discover a student who actually cares about improving their work. If not, they should be.

One of the simplest ways to improve your writing is to read a wide range of different kinds of texts – from novels and newspapers to Nobel-prizewinning essays. Try to develop an eye for the different styles and structures these texts use. As you improve your language skills, you will also sharpen your understanding of your own subject. Good reading and writing skills are not an optional extra to your studies; they are right at the core of the education system. Make these a priority and you will quickly become a more perceptive reader. Soon you will also be able to express your own ideas with force and clarity. I cannot promise that all your writing problems will disappear overnight, but I can assure you that once you start paying more attention to this element of your work, you will begin to find the feedback you receive more useful, and you will pick up new skills in handling language and forming arguments. After that, it is up to you to make sure you have something interesting to say.

part

one

where do I start?

01

before
you begin

In this chapter you will learn:
- why your course has written work
- what skills you need to get started.

What are essays for?

Essays and dissertations are so much part and parcel of life at school, college and university that it is easy to forget why they are there. Of course, there are other ways of assessing students' work; nowadays in many subjects you are just as likely to be asked to take an online multiple-choice test or create a learning log as to hand in a long piece of written text. However, the essay remains one of the most effective ways of assessing your understanding of your subject. It will test the extent of your knowledge. It will also test key intellectual abilities, including:

- ordering material effectively to form an argument
- applying an appropriate methodology
- expressing your own ideas and judgements
- providing detailed sources for your information
- presenting information clearly and accurately.

So, the essay does not just show your marker what you know about the topic of the essay. He or she will also end up with a fairly clear picture of how you know what you know, and how well you know it.

There are many different kinds of essay. A mid-term assessment is likely to be a piece of written work of around 1,500 to 3,000 words, focusing on a specific area of your course. Chapter 03 looks at some of the different kinds of essays you might be asked to write. At some point in your studies you will probably also have to sit exams, which may involve short essays of a few pages, planned and executed in a high-pressure situation. Your programme of study may also include a dissertation, a long piece of work on a larger project, researched and written over a period of weeks or months. Later in this book, I will have some specific things to say about exams and dissertations, but mostly I will use the term 'essay' to cover all of these, as the basic rules apply to all of them. If you carry on to do postgraduate research or aim for a career in a college or university, the essay-length article will be the most common form that you use to publish your results in academic journals. Conference papers, book reviews and chapters in theses or scholarly books follow very much the same form. Your tutor is probably at work on one of these right now, and may be finding it as troublesome as you found your last essay – which is always a comforting thought.

So, like it or loathe it, the essay in all its forms remains the workhorse of intellectual life – and with good reason. Ever since Plato started writing down Socrates' conversations with his followers in the fourth century BC, readers and writers in the Western tradition have seen the process of acquiring knowledge as a dialogue or a discussion. There is always more than one way of looking at an issue, and in order to come to a judgement about which view is best, one needs to create a space in which conflicting ideas can be expressed and weighed up. This process is roughly what goes on in seminars and tutorials when students and tutors discuss a problem or theory. It is also what happens when you get two or more university lecturers in the same room, sometimes with spectacular results. It is no accident that the core structure of an essay is often referred to as the 'argument'. When this discussion happens on paper in a polite and organized way, it becomes an essay. The job of your essay or dissertation is to show what you have learned, put it in the context of your discipline, demonstrate the soundness of your knowledge, and weigh up its value.

What are you studying?

This may seem an odd question to ask at this stage. However, it is very easy to get so caught up in the particular essay you are writing that you can lose sight of its role in your larger programme of study. In later sections I will have more to say about tailoring your work to fit the conventions and expectations of your discipline, but at this stage you should understand why you need to write an essay at all.

Although it may not seem obvious to you, your essay has been set as an integral part of your course or degree programme. Committees have deliberated about its length and form, and the questions are likely to have been approved by several members of staff, possibly even by experts from another university. Your essay is a vital component in your course of study, not a random IQ test. It can be very helpful to stop and think for a few minutes about why your tutors have set an essay, rather than a different kind of assessment, and about which elements they are testing.

Ask yourself

- What is this course or module about?
- Why is this course or module valuable as part of my programme of study?
- What can I learn about my subject by writing this essay?
- What skills can I develop by writing this essay?

In modern academic life, issues about core skills and content in courses are quite closely regulated, which is why at the beginning of every term you will be given a course handbook or referred to a webpage explaining what your course is about. These do not often make riveting reading. However, they can be a valuable source of inside information about what markers want to see in written work. Try to find the section that is about 'learning outcomes' or 'aims and objectives'. This offers a kind of X-ray view of your course. It allows you to see under the surface and get a picture of what your tutors and lecturers consider the essential framework.

In the description of the course there is usually a section about 'knowledge' or 'content', which focuses on the kind of material you should have learned over the term. For example: an understanding of the place of class and gender in nineteenth-century culture, or the effect of carbon dioxide levels on tree growth, or the usefulness of object teaching in primary schools. There is also usually a section about 'skills' or 'outcomes', which focuses on things your tutors want you to be able to do. For example: evaluate a range of historical sources and secondary reading, or gather and analyse data effectively, or collate and evaluate a series of case studies. One of the things your essay should do is show that you have successfully engaged with the course. So, try to keep these aims and outcomes in mind as you write, and let your marker see that you have been developing skills and knowledge in the relevant areas.

What skills will you need?

Your course guide can also give you a good idea of what you will need to do to plan a successful piece of written work. If you are expected to evaluate a range of historical sources and secondary reading, you will obviously need to factor in a lot of time in the library. If you are gathering and analysing data, you may need to spend less time in the book stacks, but more time thinking out a questionnaire for a survey, finding candidates to interview, adding up the results and designing graphs and charts. Some of these skills will be specific to your discipline. This book will not be able to help you much with these. You are much better getting expert advice from your lecturers and tutors on the technicalities of your subject. However, there are some activities that are much the same whatever you are studying.

Every piece of written work requires:

- **planning:** choosing a topic and deciding how to approach it
- **research:** gathering the right kind of material
- **thought:** analysing this material and forming a conclusion
- **more planning:** deciding how to present your ideas and results
- **writing:** putting it into words
- **editing:** rereading to correct mistakes and improve presentation.

These are essential for almost any project, but it is remarkable how many students think they can get by just on research and writing. Most essays and dissertations show evidence of some thought, in varying quantities, but planning and editing are often squeezed out because they take a lot of extra time. There is always some smart cookie in a class who can start on an piece of work two days before the deadline and get a decent result. However, these essays hardly ever get the highest marks. Even when written with flair and style, they are usually poorly organized, full of surface errors, and could have been a lot better given a bit more effort. First-class work is always the product of careful thought and attention to detail. Academics often describe high-quality work as 'rigorous', meaning that you can see a probing and hardworking mind at work. This does not mean it is dull – far from it. Often it is the mix of precision and originality that really makes an essay sparkle.

Get organized

If you are serious about improving your work, you should get going early. If you have a job or family commitments, plan your time very carefully. Try to leave some extra time to allow for something unexpected. If you have small children they will almost certainly need to be off school or nursery for a few days just when you need a good stretch of time in the library. If you have a job, you will inevitably be called in to cover someone else's sick leave or holiday, just when you are trying to write up your project results. Some forward thinking can help you make the most of your limited time. Start much earlier than you think is necessary.

To improve your work, you might not need to spend much more time actually writing than you have until now. However, you should factor in extra time for planning your research, time for planning the structure of your essay, and time for editing your work once you have written a draft version. Add all of this time up and then double it. Finding good resources online or in the library always takes longer than you think, and tidying up typos and references is a never-ending task. If you do have the project finished a few days before the deadline, you can leave it sitting for a day or two and then go back to it with fresh eyes. I guarantee you will find something you want to change or correct when you reread it.

> **Top tip**
>
> At the start of term write a list or draw a chart with the due dates of all your assignments. Stick it up over your desk, on the fridge or beside the mirror. Think ahead and leave plenty of time for each project.

Honing your study skills takes years and, to be honest, some highly successful academics never quite learn to organize their time efficiently or meet all their deadlines. But on the whole it will help your written work if you are organized, approach the task in a methodical manner, get hold of the right resources early on, and leave yourself enough time to actually enjoy the process of learning and writing. After all, you chose your course, and you, or someone near and dear to you, may be paying a good deal of money for the privilege of studying. So, you might as well make the most of it.

The following chapters will give you extensive advice on the areas of study skills that relate to writing assessed work. If you would like more advice on other aspects of studying, such as taking lecture notes, using technology, tackling lab work, or revising effectively, there are many published guides to the subject. Try *Teach Yourself Good Study Skills* by Bernice Walmsley. However, the next section of this book will help you to make use of one of the most valuable resources for your work: your tutor.

Quick fix

- Think about your subject and why you chose to study it. Consider why written work is important as a part of your overall programme of study. Identify skills which you should develop.

- Think about your course or module. Look at your course guide to find out what the main themes and learning outcomes of the course are. How does your essay connect with these themes and outcomes?

- If you are juggling work or family commitments with your studies, plan your time very carefully. Aim to be finished a few days before the deadline to allow for something unexpected to crop up. It probably will.

- Build in extra time for planning your project, finding good resources and editing your work once you have written the essay. Many students skimp on these elements of essay writing, and it shows.

02

how markers think

In this chapter you will learn:
- how to work out what your marker is looking for
- what sort of help you can expect from your tutor.

Writing for your reader

All writing, whether it is a magazine article, a sonnet or a technical manual on how to build a racing car, should be angled towards a particular audience. Newspaper companies spend thousands of pounds on marketing consultants who research the income bracket, shopping habits and leisure pursuits of their readers, in the competitive battle to keep circulation numbers high. Similarly, when writers approach publishers with an idea for a new publication, one of the first questions they have to answer is: 'Who will read this book?' There is no point producing material that does not appeal to its target audience. It simply will not sell.

Ask yourself the same question: Who will read my essay? Much of the time your work will be marked by your own tutor, but it is also likely to be double-marked by other members of staff who teach on the course. Sometimes marking is reviewed or 'moderated' by other members of staff in the department. This involves checking a random sample of essays. All marking within a higher education institution is subject to review by external examiners from other institutions, who have the job of making sure that your tutors are marking fairly and consistently.

So, you cannot assume that your tutor will be the only person who will read your work. You need to construct a general profile of the kind of reader who might make a judgement on your writing, and keep this ideal reader in mind as you write. Chapter 11 will give you some more advice on how to develop the right tone of voice or 'register' for this reader. If this sounds daunting, remember that markers (with a few fierce exceptions) like to see students do well. If you can avoid annoying them with basic errors and sloppy presentation, you are likely to get a very fair hearing.

Your marker

Your target reader will be a highly educated professional person with considerable training in your field. They are likely to have a PhD or a similar postgraduate qualification, or they may be in the later stages of working towards one. They will probably be somewhere between their late twenties and their early sixties. Most academics could earn more money if they worked in the corporate world, but they choose not to. This suggests that they are highly motivated and are passionately interested in their subject. However, they are unlikely to spend all of their time teaching and marking. Even full-time academic staff have other kinds of duties. Many of them consider their research activities their priority, and all of them have more administrative work than they would like. Despite this, many genuinely enjoy teaching and approach a pile of mid-term assessments with optimism.

This optimism waxes and wanes as the marker works their way through the pile, and pours out yet another mug of coffee. Somewhere in the middle of this process they will arrive at your essay. It is important to remember that although you may have spent days and weeks on your assignment, and invested a lot of energy in the project, your marker sees it initially as just another set of stapled sheets in the pile. They are likely to spend somewhere between 20 minutes and an hour on it, depending on its length and quality. You have only a short time in which to impress. What do they want to see?

What markers look for

Whatever subject you are studying and whatever topic you choose for your assignment, it is likely to be assessed according to the same basic principles. Somewhere on your college or university website, there will be a list of marking criteria, which lets you see the rules by which markers operate. At my own university there are five basic criteria, which apply to every subject. Each piece of written work is judged on:

1 Understanding and appreciation of the issue(s) raised by the question or topic.
2 Knowledge of and skill in using and, where appropriate, analysing particular concepts and/or sources.
3 Relevance and fullness of the answer.
4 Use of arguments and/or evidence to support observations and conclusions.
5 Ability to express ideas and/or arguments clearly, cogently and coherently.

The list your marker will use probably looks very similar. Markers do not always sit with this list in front of them, but these criteria are right at the heart of how they will evaluate your work. A really good piece of work should excel in all of these areas, not just in three or four of them.

The item on the list that is to do with expression and/or presentation often comes at the bottom of such lists of marking criteria. But remember that when your marker picks up your essay, they will start making a judgement about your abilities in this area before they have finished the first paragraph. Spelling mistakes or weird fonts on the cover sheet do not help either. Just as you would want to tidy up before going on a date or giving a presentation, it is important to make a good first impression with written work. Even a highly intelligent piece of work can get off on the wrong foot if it is poorly presented and does not read well from the start. See Chapters 09 and 10 for more advice on making a good first impression.

Many departments reserve up to 20 per cent of the marking scale for issues of presentation and expression. This is the difference between a first-class mark and a very average second-class. Serious problems with grammar and referencing can obscure your argument so badly that you may fail the assessment altogether. Some departments, especially in science-based subjects, say that they do not penalize poor grammar and spelling 'where the meaning is clear'. But the fact is that a cleanly presented essay with good grammar and spelling is always going to do better than a scruffy, poorly written one with similar content. If you want to pick up some extra marks for your work, this is probably the easiest place to start. Good presentation skills are also highly valued by employers in an age when nobody seems to know where to put apostrophes any more. So any effort in this area will be time well spent.

> **Top tip**
>
> If your essay is going to be late, let your tutor know as early as you can. If you are ill or have a good reason, you should be able to get an extension, but it always looks better if you ask before the due date.

Many departments now ask students to submit work with a printed cover sheet attached. This usually has a declaration which you must sign saying that the essay is all your own work and that any sources have been acknowledged. This should alert you to the fact that universities and colleges take this issue quite seriously. Plagiarism, which is the use of anyone else's work without due acknowledgement, is considered a serious offence in the academic world (see Chapter 18), and it can lead to a student being thrown out of university. However, you should not panic about this. If you understand the basic rules of referencing, it is quite difficult to plagiarize by accident. Departmental cover sheets, like course guides, can also be a good source of information on what markers value. Many have a checklist of categories such as 'structure of argument', 'use of sources', 'depth of research' and 'quality of expression'. The number of ticks in boxes does not always correspond mathematically to the mark you get, but the categories listed will give you a handy guide to the criteria which your marker is likely to have in mind while marking.

Feedback

Markers vary hugely in the amount and quality of feedback which they give. It is not necessarily a bad thing if your essay comes back full of notes in the margin. This probably means that you have a highly engaged marker, who is likely to be exactly the kind of person who can help you develop your writing skills. Even if they have given you a less than brilliant mark, this could be the start of an upward trend in your work. Individual feedback is probably the best tool for improving your writing.

Make sure you read all the feedback you get, not just the summarizing comments. Sometimes the most pithy remarks are the little queries and sarcastic comments in the margin. Try not to take offence if your marker has scored out some of your pet phrases or has altered your sentence structure. The chances are that they are trying to show you how you could make your language cleaner and sharper, or how to use a more appropriate register for academic writing. Pay particular attention if the same comments crop up repeatedly, especially if you are getting the same feedback from more than one marker. If this is the case, something is definitely wrong. The golden rule of capitalizing on essay feedback is to reread the comments from the previous essay before you start the next one. You will be less likely to make the same mistakes all over again, and you will be able to develop your thinking and writing skills in the right direction.

Alternatively, your essay may come back with very few notes in the margin. This can mean one of several things: your essay may be so good that it does not need much correcting; you may have a marker who cannot be bothered to offer much constructive advice; or you may have a good-natured marker who has come to the conclusion that a lot of students simply do not read comments in the margin. Whatever your marker has put on your paper, you are entitled to discuss your work with them. Some departments have a policy of handing back essays individually, using this as a chance for a one-to-one chat with the student about their work. If you are in one of these departments, count yourself lucky. This practice is becoming rarer and rarer. However, even very large and busy departments have a policy of making staff available to see students to discuss their progress. If you would like more feedback than you are getting, or do not understand what your marker has said, it is worth going to see them.

Ask yourself

- If you were marking your own essay, what would you be looking for?
- What kind of feedback would help you improve your writing?
- If you could ask an international expert in your field one question, what would it be?
- What did your marker say about your last essay?

Discussing your work

Staff usually have office hours, once or twice a week, in which they have an 'open door' to students. If you want to see your tutor, try to go during their office hour, or email to arrange a time, rather than just dropping in when it suits you. The worst time to attempt to catch your tutor is at ten to the hour, when they are likely to be on the point of getting ready to teach another class. If you want to talk about your work in some depth, leave your essay with your tutor and arrange to come back in a day or two. Remember that the last time they saw it, probably a couple of weeks ago, it was in a pile of other papers on similar topics, so they may want to read it through again before discussing it.

Talking about your work with your tutor is most productive when you have read through the feedback carefully and when you come with some specific questions about how you could do better. Try not to ask, 'Why did I only get a third-class mark?' You will get a more helpful answer if you ask, 'How should I have structured my answer?' or 'Did I use the right kind of sources?' Do not attempt to convince your tutor that your way of doing things was right after all. Try to find out exactly where things went wrong and what you should do next time to put them right. If you really want to improve your work, ask if there is a member of staff or a study skills unit on campus who can help with your writing skills. Study skills tutors are often seen as emergency support for struggling students, but they are sometimes willing to help mid-stream students who believe they can do better. If you have medical or emotional problems that may interfere with your work, make sure you tell your tutor. Most colleges and universities can offer support.

A good way to get the most out of your tutor is to ask them to recommend one or two books or articles that might broaden your understanding of your subject. Most tutors love to be asked this question, and you can get some very useful answers. Make sure you follow this up by actually reading what they recommend. Later in the term, tell your tutor how you got on with these texts, or cite one in your next assignment – if it is relevant. This lets your tutor know you are serious about putting in the extra effort to improve your work, which can lead to a good working relationship in the future. Whenever you go to see your tutor, do not be embarrassed to take a notebook with you and write things down, as you probably won't remember everything your tutor says. And try not to outstay your welcome. A student who takes up the whole office hour every time they drop in can make the heart of even the kindest tutor sink like a stone.

If you felt the mark for your essay was unfair, and talking to your tutor does not put your mind at rest, you are usually entitled to request a remark. Sometimes, if the work has been double-marked already, this is not possible. Speak to the course co-ordinator or your advisor of studies. However, use this option only in emergencies. Word gets around a department very quickly when students start complaining about marks. If you do this more than once, you will not make yourself very popular. If all your marks seem unfair, perhaps the problem is really that you need to revise your ideas about your work. Remember that you have lots of pieces of work to complete throughout your programme of study, and external examiners are there to pick up any rogue marks if they affect your final overall result.

Discussing your work with your tutor may throw up some unexpected results. My mother tells the story of when she was a student in Edinburgh in the 1950s. Having had an essay marked, she found there was one comment scribbled in the margin which she could not read. She showed it to several friends, none of whom could decipher it. In the end she plucked up her courage and took it back to her tutor to ask him what he had written. He looked a little sheepish and replied, 'It says, "I cannot read your handwriting".'

Quick fix

- Think about who will mark your work and what they will expect to see.
- Check the marking criteria for your college or university. This can give you some useful information about what aspects of your work you might need to improve to boost your grades.
- Read all the feedback you get on your essay. Read it again before you write the next piece of work. This will help you to avoid repeating mistakes and to build on the advice your marker gave.
- Do not be too shy to go and see your tutor to discuss your work. That is part of their job. Ask specific questions and take a note of the answers.

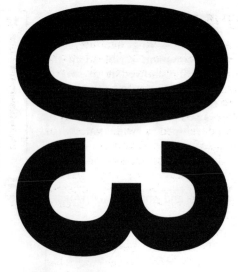

03

know your assignment

In this chapter you will learn:
- about different types of coursework
- what skills are needed for each type of essay.

What sort of essay is this?

In the opening chapters we have been looking at the things that all essays have in common. We have explored the importance of good writing, the basic organizational and academic skills you will need to construct an essay, and the criteria by which it will be judged. However, there is no point pretending that all essays are the same. Different disciplines need to test different kinds of intellectual abilities and have developed a wide variety of projects and assignments to focus on these. If you are doing a joint degree, or if you are studying at a university or college where you have the opportunity to select courses from a variety of subjects, you have probably noticed already that different departments expect slightly different things from you. Even if you are working within one area of study, you are likely to be asked to complete several different kinds of assignment throughout your programme of study. This chapter will help you think about what sort of essay you are writing and what areas of your knowledge and skill it will test. Larger projects and dissertations often require a student to bring several different skills or areas of knowledge together, so it can be helpful to see a dissertation as a blend or sequence of several kinds of essay. I will be looking at how this process works in the next chapter, along with some advice about exams.

When is it due?

One of the most important things you should know about your essay is when and where you have to hand it in. You cannot find out too early. Make sure you check the submission dates and regulations for your course as soon as it starts. This information is usually in the course guide or on the webpage. You should also check what happens if your essay is late, or if you are ill. Many colleges or universities require you to hand in a medical certificate if you are too ill to complete written work on time. Find out how to do this before it happens. It is not much fun trying to find your way through the system with a temperature and a sore throat. If you do not know the regulations, check them now.

Top tip

If you have two essays due on the same day, do one at a time. Set yourself a deadline a week early for one of them and stick to it as firmly as if it were the real deadline. You do not need to hand in the essay early. If you have time, you can reread it the day before the official deadline and correct a few more mistakes.

Formal essay

The formal essay is the type of assessment most commonly set in colleges and universities, especially in the areas of arts, humanities, social sciences and education. However, you may also have to write formal essays for courses in sciences and medicine. The term 'essay' was invented by the French writer Montaigne in 1580 for his collection of *Essais*. In French the word means 'attempts' and it can be useful to think of your essay as an opportunity to 'try out' an idea or theory. The term was first used in English by Francis Bacon in the late sixteenth century and has been around ever since. It is usually used to describe a balanced, methodical, but not exhaustive, discussion of a single issue or question in a short written form. There is also an 'informal' essay form, in which the writer discusses a subject in a relaxed, personal, light-hearted way, much like a newspaper column. Try to remember that an academic essay is of the formal variety. No wise-cracks, please.

Formal essays can vary in length, but at undergraduate level they are most likely to be 1,500 to 3,000 words. The standard structure of the formal essay has its roots in Classical rhetoric in which a speaker offered a speech in five parts:

- **introduction**: outlining the topic in hand
- **statement**: presenting one side of the argument
- **counterstatement**: presenting the other side of the argument
- **analysis**: weighing up which side is best
- **conclusion**: stating the outcome.

This pattern is also at the core of political life and the legal system. So, it is no surprise to find it at work in the academic world as well. In Chapter 07, you will find some more detailed advice on how to structure your material to fit this kind of essay form. At this stage, however, you should note the need for both a balance between conflicting views and a conclusion about which one comes out on top. Although you should consider a range of perspectives in a formal essay, ultimately your job is to weigh up which is most valid. Do not run away from this responsibility.

Some study guides draw a distinction between the 'informational' essay and the 'persuasive' essay. This distinction is unhelpful, as a formal essay is always a blend of information and persuasion, and it is often very difficult to tell where one stops and the other starts. However, you will have to make a value judgement about how much of each to include, based on your subject and your specific question. At each stage of the essay you should refer to evidence which supports both your own viewpoint and those of others. You should also analyse and evaluate the value of this evidence. Ultimately, the job of the formal essay is to offer a measured discussion on a subject which is in some way open to debate or interpretation, and to draw a reasonable conclusion. It is designed to test your knowledge of the subject, your ability to gather and evaluate evidence, your powers of logical analysis, and your handling of language. It is an all-round intellectual workout.

Literature review

Some essay forms are designed to develop specific skills. The literature review is used in a variety of disciplines to teach students how to engage with the published scholarship on a particular subject. This assignment usually involves summarizing a number of publications and discussing how these support or contradict one another. You may be asked to compare two texts, or you may be asked to present a spectrum of views from a variety of scholars and sources. In this case it can help to think of the review as a round-table discussion on the subject, with yourself in charge. Which experts should you invite to create a lively and probing debate?

For example, your review might include:

- a seminal text establishing the boundaries of the discipline
- a recent text on your topic by an eminent scholar in the field
- a review criticizing or praising the newer text
- a journal article exploring the topic from a different perspective
- a theorized discussion of the terminology used in the discipline

- an online journal article outlining a new project which promises to complete more research in the area, thus moving the debate forward.

There will be other combinations which work just as well. Whatever you choose, make sure you use reputable, scholarly sources, especially if you are finding things on the internet. (See Chapter 06 for more advice on finding and choosing sources.) A mix of books, journals and internet journals usually creates a good balance, but this may vary from subject to subject. Ask your tutor what they want to see in your review.

You do not have to agree with all the texts you discuss, but make sure that every text you cite connects tightly to the subject at the core of the assignment. Unlike the formal essay, the literature review does not call for your own judgement on the subject, although you can evaluate the rigour and impact of the texts you explore. Texts which cite one another or openly refute each other can work well together. You should make sure that the majority of your texts are up to date, but remember that ideas about the shelf-life of scholarship vary dramatically between disciplines. In science or medicine, an article may be out of date within months of publication. In literature, law or history, a book may still be considered a central piece of scholarship after 25 years. Ask your tutor for guidance on this if you are uncertain. Remember, the review is designed to teach you how to find, digest and evaluate scholarly literature in your field, and to introduce you to a range of views on the subject you are studying.

Project report

If you are studying a subject with an element of practical research, you will be asked to write project reports. These are essential for lab work, field work and survey work in a variety of subjects from microbiology to psychology. Most scientific journal articles are structured in the form of the project report, so mastering this kind of assignment is a key skill for many students. The project report should explain what your project was about, how you went about it and what your results were. If you are working as part of a team, it should also make clear exactly what your role was within the project.

Obviously, writing the project report will be easier if you have clear notes to work from, so make sure you keep track of what is happening at all stages of the project. The report should not be a reproduction of your project diary, and you do not have to include every minute detail. However, you should include enough detail for somebody else to repeat your experiment accurately by following your report. Good technical writing should be informative and concise. Learning to select what is important is a crucial part of becoming a skilled researcher. Present your information in a straightforward, logical sequence.

A project report begins with a short abstract of 100–200 words. This should give a brief indication of the aim of the project, the methods used and the outcome. After the abstract, your introduction should explain the aims of the project and the methods and materials used. You might want to include some secondary literature at this stage to explain your use of one particular method. The main section of the report will describe the research or experiments you carried out and the results. You may want to use graphs and diagrams to display your results. Make sure these are clearly and correctly labelled, but do not leave them to speak entirely for themselves. Summarize what they show and explain the significance of this. (See Chapter 10 for more advice on presenting visual material.) You will then need to discuss and analyse your results, referring to other research in the area if appropriate. Lastly, state your conclusion.

In the discussion, it may also be helpful to evaluate the effectiveness of the method you used for your project. If something went wrong in the project, or you did not get the result that you expected, try to analyse why this happened and suggest other approaches that could be taken in future in order to overcome this problem. This shows that you are thinking creatively about your work instead of simply following a set procedure. (For more advice on structuring project reports see Chapter 07.)

Remember that your potential reader is not just your project supervisor. You should not assume that your reader has seen the project unfold step by step, so explain what happened clearly and confidently. Do not explain terms that are common currency in your subject, but try to make the report simple enough so that another student at your level of study would understand how your project had been carried out.

The purpose of the project report is not simply to show that you and your project team arrived at the 'right answer' during your research. The report should show:

- that you carried out your project using appropriate methods
- that you applied these carefully
- that you kept careful records
- that you analysed your data sensibly
- that you took account of relevant scholarship
- that you were aware of other methods or approaches that could have been used.

These are all key skills in academic research. Let your marker see that you are developing these abilities.

> **Ask yourself**
>
> - What kind of assignment am I writing?
> - What are the key skills for this assignment?
> - Why are these skills important in my discipline?

Learning log

A learning log, as its name suggests, is a record or diary of your learning. You are most likely to be asked to keep a learning log in subjects such as teaching, nursing or social work, where you are learning skills of professional practice. It is also beginning to appear as a course requirement in other academic subjects, but anybody can keep a learning log. This can be a good way to improve your study skills and make you a more effective learner. The log is designed to encourage you to evaluate your own progress and to learn from your experience. It can be a particularly useful exercise alongside a work placement on a ward, in a school or in the community. Sometimes the learning log will be formally assessed and graded, but more often this is a fairly informal type of project. It may be used as a discussion document with your supervisor or advisor during an end-of-term review. Alternatively, it may be up to you to assess whether it has been helpful or not.

The key skill for a learning log is self-evaluation, also called reflective practice or critical reflection. Many careers require regular self-evaluation, so this is a good skill to learn now. Your learning log is not just a record of what you did or the knowledge you acquired; it is an opportunity to reflect on your learning experience, how you felt about it, and how you can develop skills in the future. You may find it helpful to have a checklist of questions which you work through at each entry so that you can see how you are progressing in each area. These questions might include:

- What did I do?
- What theory did I put into practice?
- What ideas did it throw up?
- How did it make me feel?
- How well/badly did it go?
- What did I learn about my subject?
- What did I learn about myself?
- What skills do I need to develop?
- What will I do differently next time?
- How have I progressed since last time?

Do not be disheartened if you find yourself going over similar ground many times. It can take a long time to learn new skills and to develop your confidence in using them, especially if you are working with children, patients or clients. The learning log can help you to keep track of the different approaches that you have tried and how well these worked for you. When things go badly, look back through the log to remind yourself of the times when you did well. Try to stay positive. Do not let the learning log become a document of despair and self-pity. Be honest about the areas where you need to improve, but focus on your strengths and develop strategies for using them.

Case study

Case studies are used in many different disciplines to explore the impact of a situation or a methodological approach on a particular person or group. You may be asked to write a case study based on a practical project in which you have been involved, or you may be asked to research a documented event through source material. In some exercises you could be asked to compare two similar cases. The hallmark of a case study is that you are writing about a genuine situation involving real people. Subjects for this type of project could include: a fraud trial; a small business venture; the impact of environmental change on an island community in the Indian Ocean; or the usefulness of speech therapy for a child with learning difficulties. The benefit of a case study is that it allows you to see theoretical ideas working in the real world. However, the difficulty with a case study can be knowing how much you should generalize from one particular situation. The exercise is partly designed to test your awareness of this problem.

As with a project report, it is important to offer a balance of information and analysis in a case study. Make sure you are thoroughly familiar with the facts of your case and with the theoretical method that you plan to use to analyse it. Think critically about both these elements. Do you have all the information you need? Is your method appropriate for this particular case? You should give a summary of the narrative of the case in the introduction. However, in the main body of the text do not devote all your energy and word count to describing what happened. Remember that your task is to analyse the situation. You should:

- demonstrate your knowledge of the case
- look for the causes of events
- relate what happened to relevant theories in your discipline
- assess the effects of any actions or developments
- show what can be learned from this particular case
- propose solutions or further research.

If the case study is connected to a project in which you have been personally active, or if you have been working in a team, it can be helpful to include a reflective section in which you assess what you contributed and what you have learned. See the section above on learning logs for some ideas about how to approach this.

Close reading

The close reading is a standard form of assessment in subjects which depend upon a lot of textual sources, such as literature, history and religious studies. In this kind of exercise you are given a short piece of text, which you are expected to analyse both for content and for style of expression. This exercise can also be called critical analysis, textual analysis, practical criticism, exegesis, or a gobbet question. In case you were wondering, a 'gobbet' is an Old English word that refers to a tasty morsel plucked out of a pot of stew. This word is often used by historians to refer to a particularly interesting section of a historical document which is worth chewing over – which is actually quite a good way to think about this kind of project.

You may be given a 'seen' close reading, which is a section of a text that you have already read and know something about. In this case, you are probably being encouraged to discuss the importance of the set passage to the text as a whole, and to consider the passage as a representative example of the written style of the whole text. It may also be appropriate to discuss the context and impact of the text, and anything you know about its composition and background. Alternatively, you may be presented with an 'unseen' close reading. In this case, you are probably being asked to demonstrate your skills of reading and linguistic analysis. You may be expected to recognize a particular kind of text, such as a sonnet, a political speech or a passage of scripture. You should also explore how the language of the passage elicits a particular response or demonstrates a particular worldview.

Both kinds of close reading are designed to test your awareness of how words create and reflect emotions and ideologies. Avoid speculating about things that are not in the text, or guessing who wrote it, unless you know for sure. Tie everything you say back to specific things in the passage. Make sure you do not just discuss what the passage says. Look at how this is expressed. Ask yourself:

- What does this text reveal about its own origins and context?
- What sort of reader does it imply or assume?
- What ideas or questions does it raise?
- How does it make me feel?
- Which words or phrases seem most important or effective?
- Does it use a particular style of expression, for example, formal, legal, conversational, biblical or poetic?
- Are there any recurring patterns or strategies within the passage?
- Is the language concrete and particular or abstract and general?

All of these questions can help you to grasp the key aims and assumptions within the text. Pay special attention to anything that seems irrelevant or out of place, such as metaphors and similes, adjectives and adverbs, colours, inaccuracies, names of historical figures, comments in brackets, odd spellings or punctuation. Has anything important or obvious been left unsaid? These can all be valuable clues as to how the text is functioning.

This kind of question is often used as an exam question, so it is a good idea to practise your close-reading skills before the day. Take a page of a key text in your subject and work through it carefully. There is more advice on how to structure your material for a close reading answer in Chapter 07, and there is a sample answer in Chapter 08. Learning to be a shrewd, critical reader is also one of the best ways of sharpening up your own writing. As you begin to recognize the strategies which other writers use, see what you can learn about your own style and about how to make language work more effectively.

Quick fix

- Think about your assignment. What kind of essay have you been asked to write? Is it a formal essay, literature review, project report, learning log, case study, close reading, or something else?

- What skills will your assignment test? Check your course guide again to remind yourself which skills are at the core of your course. Think about how your assignment has been designed to develop these skills.

- When and where do you have to hand in your essay? What happens if it is late or you are ill? If you don't know, find out now.

- Plan your research and reading schedule to fit the kind of assignment you have been set. Get an appropriate balance between gathering and analysing information, library time and writing-up time.

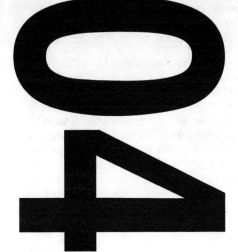

04

exams and dissertations

In this chapter you will learn:
- how to handle exams
- how to apply your essay skills to your dissertation.

Adapt and survive

Some students are very capable and confident with essays but come apart at the seams when they are asked to sit exams or to handle a long project. It can help to remember that exams and dissertations are basically testing the same skills as essays, but in a concentrated or expanded form. The exam question is likely to be a shorter, quicker version of one of the types of essay discussed in the previous chapter, while a dissertation is usually a longer version of one of these, or a combination of several. Adapt the skills that you have learned from and practised in your essays, and you will find that exams and dissertations no longer seem so intimidating

Exam skills

The formal essay is the most common type of essay question in an exam setting. However, you should never assume that this is what you will get. Check your course guide and talk to your tutor. You should be given very clear advice before the exam on the kind of questions that will come up, but sometimes you do have to ask.

Even though an exam question will be shorter and more rushed then an essay, it is testing the same skills. So, if you are asked to write a formal essay answer, remember that your marker still wants to see that classic structure of introduction, two or more views on the topic, a weighing up of the evidence, and a conclusion. A close reading should still focus on significant details and how the language of the passage works, and so on. However, exams are also testing your ability to work at speed and under pressure. Your marker wants to see that you can think clearly and can select and order material relevant to the question. So, read your question carefully and make sure you answer it. (See Chapter 05 for more advice about reading questions.) Remember, length is not everything. It is better to write a well-planned, tightly focused answer in the correct format, than to splurge everything you know about a subject on to the paper. Some careful planning both before and during the exam can help you here.

Planning for exams

When you are revising for the exam, think carefully about the types of skills your marker wants you to demonstrate in your answer. This can be a good time to go back and look at the course aims or learning outcomes in the course guide. Try to focus your answer towards these aims and outcomes. In the exam you will have to make decisions quickly. Knowing the course aims and outcomes can help you to choose which bits of information to use and how to present them.

Make sure you take a few minutes to make a plan for your answer. As a marker of many exam scripts, I can tell you that the best answers usually have a plan on the first page of the exam booklet. Put a line through any planning material in your script, so that your marker knows this page should not be marked. A plan will help to keep you on track as you write. It also gives you somewhere to jot down notes of relevant material you want to use. Under exam pressure it can be easy to forget something that seemed crystal clear 15 minutes ago. So, make a quick note when you think of something.

As in essays, you should avoid using bullet points and lists, even if you have used these to help yourself remember material. Remember that in an exam you are not just regurgitating all the information you have in your head; you are answering a question, which involves analysis, reasoning and the careful ordering of material. Construct a logical argument in a clear, concise manner and draw a conclusion.

Think smart

Look at old exam papers for your course to get an idea of the kinds of questions that will come up. This is always helpful. Make sure you also have a good look at the 'rubric'. This is the set of instructions at the front or top of the exam paper. These can give some valuable clues about what your marker wants to see. You should also read this carefully on the day of your own exam. Sometimes it may be slightly different from last year's paper.

If you are sitting an 'open book' exam, in which you are allowed to bring in certain set texts, make sure you use them. Allowing you to have these texts in the exam hall is a sure sign that you are expected to know your way around them and to quote from them. Demonstrate your ability to do this. Give clear references and page numbers.

Similarly, if you are allowed to bring in protractors, rulers and coloured pencils, this probably means that you are expected to be able to present some of your material in graph or diagram form. Be prepared for this, and always check your numbers carefully. It is easy to slip up under pressure. As in essays, connect your visual material to your text. You should explain and analyse the information contained in your graphs and diagrams.

Markers are usually fairly tolerant about minor errors and slips of the pen in exams, so long as your meaning is clear. However, you can do yourself a big favour by handing in a paper that is neat, readable and written with style and accuracy. If you usually type lecture notes and essays, give yourself some practice writing longhand, and make sure your handwriting is legible. It may make sense to you, but can anybody else decipher it? Always think about who might read your work and make life easy for them. Persistent spelling mistakes and grammatical errors mar an exam paper as much as they do an essay, so do not be in such a rush that you forget how to spell Hemingway or Savonarola or Heisenberg. Try to leave yourself a few minutes at the end of the exam to read over your answers and correct any mistakes that you find.

Finally, bring a spare pen. It is amazing how many people forget.

Ask yourself

- What kind of exam question am I expecting?
- What essay skills can I adapt for use in my exam?
- Can anybody read my handwriting?

Dissertation

Writing a dissertation can seem a daunting task. This is likely to be the longest piece of work you have tackled so far. It is also likely to count for a considerable proportion of your final result. This may be the first time that you have taken on a project on a different topic from any of your classmates. However, there is no need to panic. You are likely to have the expert help of a supervisor who has seen many similar projects safely to conclusion. You are also likely to be nearing the end of your programme of study. Even if you do not feel like it, you probably already have most of the abilities that you need to complete a successful dissertation. If you have been paying anything like attention over the past few months and years, you will have been quietly building up the skills and knowledge that you need for this project.

The length and form of your dissertation will depend upon the type of subject you are studying. However, it is likely to develop the essay skills that you have already learned during your studies. If most of your written work so far has been of the formal essay type, it is likely that your dissertation will be an extended version of this form. Some humanities subjects call the dissertation a 'long essay', which suggests just this. If your coursework has included a mix of assessments (for example, literature reviews, project reports and formal essays), then it is likely that your dissertation should include elements of all of these. Discuss the form of your dissertation carefully with your supervisor before you start doing your research. You will need to know what kind of material you need before you plan your project.

Top tip

Departments often keep dissertations from previous years. Ask to have a look at a first-class one to see what sort of topic it tackles, what sort of plan it follows, how it is presented and how long the bibliography is. This information will help you plan your own project.

Running your own show

Often the most satisfying aspect of a dissertation is being able to choose a topic that really interests you, and which you can tackle all by yourself. This is a great opportunity to show what you can do. Although your supervisor will try to keep you on the right track, the dissertation is partly designed to test your independence as a scholar. If you are working at Masters level, or if you are hoping to go on to further research, then the dissertation can show whether you are cut out for a career as an academic researcher – or not.

Organize your time before you start by writing a timetable for the project. Work back from the submission date and leave yourself plenty of extra time, especially in the final stages. Break the project up into workable sections and set yourself achievable targets for each stage. Work out what you need to organize in terms of practical elements, such as labwork, surveys or fieldwork. Try to get a lot of the reading done early, especially if your project includes a literature review section. This will sharpen up your own thinking on your topic and will give you some good ideas for organizing and presenting your project.

Aim to have a draft of the project completed a week or even two weeks before the deadline. It will take much longer than you think to check the manuscript, sort out glitches with printing and layout and have the dissertation bound, if required. If you have the dissertation finished early, ask a friend to read a draft copy to see if it makes sense and to spot some of the errors which you will have missed. Be prepared to return the favour. Parents, grandparents and retired schoolteachers in the house next door can also make enthusiastic proofreaders. They will probably be pleased to have been asked, and are likely to appreciate a glimpse into what you have been studying – especially if they have been paying your fees. Be prepared to buy a box of chocolates.

Ask yourself

- Have I allowed enough time for each stage of this project?
- What advice have I heard more than once from my supervisor?
- Who can I ask to proofread my dissertation?

Finding a topic

As you are likely to spend weeks, perhaps even months, working on your dissertation, it is important that you choose an area of research that you find interesting and that you feel you can handle confidently. Departments vary in the amount of freedom students are given in choosing topics, but you should work closely with your supervisor in choosing a topic and working out a question or thesis. Unless you are writing a PhD, a dissertation does not have to be a groundbreaking piece of research, but it should have some level of originality. So, work creatively with your supervisor to challenge assumptions and to create new perspectives.

Take account of any advice your supervisor gives on choosing a topic. They will have seen many projects come and go, and they are likely to know what is possible with the time and resources available. Many students at dissertation level want to take on very ambitious projects that would be more suited to a PhD project, or even a major international research project with several full-time researchers. If this applies to you, and you feel passionately about the subject, then consider applying to do research in that area – after you have finished your dissertation. At this stage it is better to choose something manageable and execute it well.

A good way to generate a topic is to think about a set of classes or an assessment which you particularly enjoyed and in which you did well. Was there anything in those classes or in that assessment on which you would have liked to have spent more time? Did any of your project reports or case studies suggest further research in a similar area that you would have liked to have followed up? Could you expand some work that you did earlier to look at a similar issue in more depth or by using a different method? Discuss with your supervisor whether you are allowed to tackle similar material twice. Some departments have strict rules about not writing on the same text, topic or case study more than once. However, it is usually possible to do something similar or in a related area. There is more advice on finding a topic in the next chapter.

If your supervisor says that they are not qualified to supervise the particular project that you want to do, then choose a different topic or ask for a different supervisor. Do not forge ahead regardless. There are no medals for bravery in dissertations. Keep in touch with your supervisor throughout the project and take their advice seriously. However brilliant your ideas may be, the fact is that your supervisor has more experience than you, and is likely to be able to help you save time and avoid simple errors. They will also be able to keep you straight on issues of presentation and referencing, which are often marked more strictly at dissertation level. So heed any advice given in this area.

Quick fix

- Get organized for exams. Double-check the date, time and venue. You cannot ace the exam if you are not there.
- Look at old papers, and think about which themes and approaches from the course are likely to come up in the exam. What are you expected to take with you? Does this give you any hints on what you should revise?
- Read exam questions carefully. Take a few minutes to plan your answer before you start writing, and jot down ideas on your planning page as you go along. Make sure you answer the question.
- Talk about your dissertation with your supervisor. Find out what structure it should have, and choose a manageable topic which you can handle in the time available.
- Start work early on your dissertation and leave lots of time for corrections. You will produce a better piece of work and will feel more satisfied with it if you have enough time to relax and enjoy working on the project.

05
questions and topics

In this chapter you will learn:
- how to read a set question
- how to choose a topic of your own.

What will I write about?

The easiest way to fail an assessment is not to answer the question. It is therefore important that you understand how your question works and what you are expected to do with it. For many assignments, you will be given an element of choice about your subject. Either you will be asked to select a question from a list, or you will be invited to suggest a topic of your own. Choosing the right subject for your essay or dissertation can be vital to success. But what is the right subject? How can you tell which topic is going to allow you to produce your best work? How can you be sure that you understand the question? This chapter will give you advice on these issues and will give you some hints about how to read the language used in essay questions. Choosing a set question is often simpler than designing your own project, so I will start with that.

Which question?

You might think that choosing a question is the first stage of your assignment. Some students pick a question from the course guide before the course has even started. However, you are probably wiser to wait and do a bit of thinking and research before you finalize your essay topic. When you read through the list of essay questions provided for your course or suggested dissertation topics, there will probably be one that jumps out at you as the most obvious or the easiest to answer. This may not be the smart one to choose. An easy question often leads to a very average answer, while something a little more challenging may allow you to produce a really top-flight piece of work. The obvious choice may also be very popular with your classmates, so you might find yourself competing with a number of other students for the relevant resources in the library.

If you are presented with a choice of several questions, it is a good idea to give serious consideration to two or even three of the questions. Try to think about how you might approach these questions and the resources you would need for each one. At this stage it is worth spending an afternoon in the library finding out which books or journals you might want to use. It can be a good idea to read a chapter or an article on each of your possible subjects, to see which one really catches your imagination and starts your ideas flowing. There is more advice on finding sources in Chapter 06. Part Four of this book will also give more advice about how to use your source material. However, at this stage you should already be thinking about which resources are available to you.

Ask yourself

- Does your library provide access to useful online resources or search engines in your area, such as Ingenta, Intute, JSTOR, LION, Project MUSE or PubMed?
- Does your library have good holdings of source material such as newspapers or periodicals that you could use?
- Could you make good use of material from a related discipline in a different section of the library?

Once you have had a look at some of the available resources it can be useful to scribble down a rough plan of how you might tackle each question. A few headings should be enough at this stage. Sometimes it is best to do this away from your books – at a café, in the bath or on the bus. That way you get a clearer view of the ideas which are beginning to form in your own head. If you are having trouble thinking up headings, or if your headings are so vague and abstract that you are not quite sure how you would approach them, then try one of your other options. Most markers like to see work that is firmly targeted on one issue rather than generalizing on large themes. So try to choose a topic that will allow you to focus on a specific area.

Broad and focused questions

It can be hard to tell which question will help you to create a good essay, but generally a focused question gives you a better chance of writing a strong, focused answer. As a rough rule of thumb, focused questions make it clear how you should approach your research and frame your answer. Broad questions are open, can be interpreted in different ways and offer little direction. For example, the following looks like an easy question on an interesting topic:

Consider the connection between marriage and money in the nineteenth century.

However, this question is almost impossible to answer well. It is very loose and does not give you a clear idea of where you should direct your energies. It is not even clear which discipline it belongs to: literature, gender studies, cultural history, sociology, or something else. 'Consider' is also a rather vague verb. It suggests that you should have a think about the topic, but it does not make it clear how you should structure your answer. What is more, the nineteenth century is a very long time. There is no chance of being able to deal with all of it in a short piece of coursework. This question gives you very little idea where to start.

On the other hand, the following looks like a harder question on a similar subject:

Assess the impact of the 1882 Married Woman's Property Act on the lives of Victorian women.

In reality, this is much easier to answer well. You are being asked to display your knowledge and understanding of the causes and effects of one particular event. You are being invited to do some reading and research on what life was like for Victorian women (but not for men or children) before and after the 1882 Act. You are still being left a fair amount of freedom about which women you want to write about and how you will structure your essay. For example, you could focus on middle-class women, or compare the lives of upper-class and working-class women. However, from the use of the phrase 'assess the impact', it is absolutely clear that your essay should form a judgement about the importance or otherwise of the 1882 Act. By looking carefully at the question you are already well on your way to planning your answer.

If all the available options on your list of course essay questions seem rather vague, or if you really want to write about a topic which has only been offered in a broad form, then you will have to do some narrowing down for yourself. One of the traditions of the formal essay, since the days of Francis Bacon, is that it can approach a large topic by focusing on a specific issue, in a manner very like a case study. So, it should be permissible to answer the first question by writing an essay about the 1882 Married Woman's Property Act, or some other pivotal event or issue. Think back over the past few weeks of your course for a specific event or issue you have studied that is of interest and which illustrates or connects to the large topic. Make it clear in your introduction that you are aware of the enormity of the topic, and explain why the element or event you will be discussing has important implications for the wider issue.

It is often a good idea to discuss this sort of strategy with your tutor in advance. Go to an office hour and take the rough plan of your essay – even if it is very rough – so that your tutor can see where you are going with your thinking. They will soon tell you if it is not going to work, and they may have some other ideas. However, a word of advice: do not change the wording of a question without discussing this with your tutor. If your tutor does agree that you can alter the wording of a question, confirm this via email and keep your tutor's response until the essay has been marked. This way both you and your tutor know exactly what you are doing and have a record of it. Do not carry out this kind of transaction with your tutor in the corridor after a lecture or seminar. They may be hungry, tired and rather preoccupied with the lesson they have just given and may quickly forget what they have agreed with you. Alternatively, your paper may be marked by some other member of staff, who does not know what was agreed. So, put it in writing if possible.

Question-speak

Some essay questions are phrased as questions; they ask what, how, where, when and why, and have a question mark at the end. For example:

Are the UN's weaknesses also its greatest assets?

What is the relevance of the artist's intention to interpreting works of art?

What does it mean to say violence is gendered?

How has the notion of the body operated in anthropology in recent years?

Such questions are usually strong, focused questions with a clear aim built into them. However, they still require some analysis and may have weaknesses. Think about each of the words in the question. They are probably all important and should direct you towards what you are expected to do.

Questions such as the first one, which contain opposites (weaknesses/assets), invite a balanced discussion giving both sides of the argument. However, the question format makes it clear that you are expected to form a judgement one way or the other. Questions such as the third one, which call attention to terms such as 'gendered', invite an exploration of the meaning and application of the word, as well as a discussion of how this connects with the subject of violence. The last question is a 'how' question, which implies a discussion of methodology, but this question requires some clarification. How recent is recent: five years, ten years, 40 years? You can ask your tutor, or you may have to make a judgement about this yourself. If this was an exam question, you would be on your own. Think carefully about what the question is asking and what the course has covered. Your answer should make clear how you have interpreted the question. Even if the question is vague, you should try to be precise.

Alternatively, many questions are phrased as instructions. These can be more tricky. For example:

Discuss Ishmael's role as narrator in *Moby Dick*.

Evaluate the importance of handcrafts in modern-day Inuit culture.

Analyse the effect of building society interest rates on London property prices since 2000.

Compare US President Woodrow Wilson's attitude to American national identity to that of President Theodore Roosevelt.

Many students pay attention to the subject of the essay but gloss over the instructions about what they are being asked to do. Make sure you read the verbs in the questions as well as the nouns. The verbs tell you what action is required. Many of these verbs belong to an academic vocabulary that can seem a little confusing, but they fall into several general groups.

- **Discuss, Explore, Consider, Examine:** These words are all likely to be used in a formal essay question to invite a thorough discussion about the topic. In this kind of question there is often some room for creativity about how you approach your subject or what you choose to focus on. However, do not be fooled into thinking that you can just raise a few issues involved in the topic and then leave it there. You still need to include evidence and analysis, and to draw a strong conclusion to make this work.

- **Analyse, Evaluate, Assess, Demonstrate, Criticize:** These terms all require a rigorous, systematic approach to your topic or project. You are being asked to show your understanding of certain processes and to form judgements about the quality of the evidence in the area of your topic. For this kind of question you need a tightly argued structure, and you may also be wise to use a methodological approach to show that you can handle your material logically and with accuracy.

- **Differentiate, Distinguish, Compare, Contrast, Relate:** These words are used in questions where you are being asked to navigate between two topics or statements. You will need to discuss both the connections and differences between the two and look at the causes and implications of these connections and differences. Do not be tempted to write a short essay on one topic followed by a short essay on the other. Keep a dialogue between the two alive throughout the essay. This will create a much stronger answer to the question.

- **Describe, Review, State, Summarize:** These terms call for an essay rich in information, but lighter on analysis. You may be asked to recount how you went about an experiment, to give an overview of the main points of a topic or argument, or to review recent literature in your field. This kind of question is testing your skills of selection and summary. Your marker wants to know if you can pick out the important points of your topic and present these clearly, logically and accurately. However, they will still expect you to sum up and conclude at the end.

- **Prove, Justify, Defend:** Provide evidence and argument to support a statement or conclusion.

- **Disprove, Refute:** Provide evidence and argument to contradict a statement or conclusion.

In addition to these terms, your question is likely to include terms specific to your subject. Every subject has its own technical language, and learning this is part of mastering your discipline. When technical terms crop up in essay questions, make sure you read them correctly and that you have a thorough grasp of what they mean. If you are a bit shaky, then look them up, ask someone for advice, or pick another question.

Choosing your own topic

Choosing your own topic is much easier if you understand how to choose and read set questions. So, if you have skipped the previous sections in this chapter, go back and read them before going on. Pay special attention to the difference between broad and focused questions. If you are invited to choose your own topic for a project, essay or dissertation, you want to set yourself a strong question. This will make it easier for you to write a strong answer. It also helps your marker to see what your main aims are. Try to construct a sharp, focused question that gives your work direction and provides some structure for your answer.

As I have said several times already in this book, an essay should show that you have been paying attention during the course and that you have engaged with the themes and methods which are being taught. So, think back over the past few weeks of the course, and remind yourself about the course aims and outcomes. Avoid a topic that takes you out of this area. Anything that grabs your attention or that stands out in your mind can be a good starting point for an essay topic.

Ask yourself

- Was there anything during the course that you particularly enjoyed, or a topic on which you would have liked to have spent more time?
- Have you been learning to apply a method or develop a research skill which you feel confident using?
- Have you come across a particular event, text or problem that illustrates one of the main themes of the course?

Remember to build on what you have been learning in class and show off your new skills and knowledge. As with choosing a set question, this can be a good time to plan a session in the library to see what resources are available and what catches your interest.

Once you have chosen a topic, do not just stop there. Think about how you are going to approach it. What methods have you been learning in class? What different kinds of approaches and resources might be useful? Have you come across a contentious statement or quote in your reading that you could use as the springboard for a discussion? Try to form an active question that will set some limits to your essay and will make it absolutely clear to your tutor what you are aiming to do. If you can form a question, using **what, how, where, when, why,** this often helps to focus your work. Just make sure that the essay which follows provides a satisfactory answer to the question. Alternatively, you can use an instruction which is appropriate to the approach you wish to take: **discuss, evaluate, compare** or **refute.** Have the courage to choose a strong verb that pushes your essay in a clear direction. It will give your essay energy and focus.

Top tip

Look after yourself. When planning for your essay or dissertation, factor in some time off. Avoid anything that will leave you with a hangover, but take a break and relax. Swimming and outdoor activities are great ways to combat stress and get the blood flowing to your brain. Eat well, drink lots of water and get some sleep. You will com back to your desk with more energy and ideas.

Quick fix

- Go to the library and do some reading/thinking/planning before you make a final decision about your question or topic. What resources are available? Which method or approach will work best for you?
- Make sure you have chosen a strong question which offers some direction for your essay.
- How does your question connect with the themes and aims of your course? What skills and knowledge will you need to answer it effectively?
- Do you understand all the terms in your question? If you are unclear about anything, look it up or ask your tutor. It is better to look a bit silly at this stage than after the event.

Try it out: Where do I start?

What kind of assignment is each of the following questions: formal essay, literature review, project report, learning log, case study or close reading?

1 Submit 200 words to your tutor on the Friday of each week of the course, outlining what you have learned and highlighting areas for future development.

2 With reference to recent reports, consider whether local authorities should ban high-calorie, low-nutrition food in school meals.

3 Write a 500-word critical analysis of Edward Thomas's poem 'Cock Crow', explaining the structure and argument of the poem, and commenting on such features as metre, rhyme, imagery and word choice.

4 Demonstrate knowledge of the peace process in one case country, using information from diverse media sources.

5 Using a survey design, investigate whether optimistic bias among level-one students is influenced by socio-economic group.

6 Review recent publications discussing methods for teaching primary school learners about environmental issues.

7 Critically appraise the potential of both quantitative and qualitative research methods in a rural social science topic.

Are the following questions broad or focused? Are there any that are basically focused, but have an element which requires clarification?

1 Explore the connection between marriage and money in Jane Austen's *Pride and Prejudice*.

2 Provide a reasoned argument for the view that exercise can reduce the risk of coronary heart disease in a population.

3 Human interaction with the environment is characterized by conflict. To what extent do you agree or disagree with this statement? Your answer will make references to specific examples. Maps, diagrams and data should be included where appropriate.

4 African socialism has become a useful omnibus label for systems of political, economic and spatial organization which vary widely in policy and practice. Discuss.

5 'Language change cannot be divorced from societal change'. With reference to the period 1750–1950, to what extent is such a statement correct?

6 Sigmund Freud wrote: 'The greater and better part of what we know of the processes in the unconscious levels of the mind is derived from the interpretation of dreams.' Discuss.

Answers can be found on pages 198–9.

part two

building your answer

06

finding the right material

In this chapter you will learn:
- how to find relevant resources in the library and online
- how to avoid weak and unreliable sources.

Choosing sources

Choosing and using sources is an integral part of studying. Some assignments are based on a handful of set texts. However, often you will be expected to find your own resources. Finding useful texts can seem difficult, especially if most of the texts recommended in your course guide have been checked out of the library. However, there is no need to panic. There are thousands of books in your college or university library. Dozens of these will be relevant to your topic. The trick is knowing where to look. Your tutor will not be impressed if you give up searching and write a superficial essay or dissertation built up of information from lecture notes and study-notes sites on the internet. However, if you are prepared to look a little bit harder online and in the library, you will find some wonderful sources, which will inform your work and give you original ideas. Try to develop your research skills and learn to look in a range of places for your material.

Academic journals

Academic journals are a key resource for students in most science and social-science subjects. Journals present peer-reviewed research. This means that the research in each of these journals has been read and evaluated by other experts in the same field. They are often published by university presses. You can therefore assume that this research has been thoroughly critiqued and checked by capable scholars. Journal articles offer up-to-date, reliable research. It is, of course, open to dispute, and it can be interesting to watch a debate about a particular problem in your discipline unfold over several months or years. Students in subjects in the arts and humanities often forget about journal articles, but they are just as useful in these areas. Journal articles are more compact, quicker to read and sometimes more interesting than full-length books. Many journal articles are now available online as digital objects months before they actually appear in print, which gives you access to very recent research.

The easiest way to find relevant information in your field is to go to an online search engine such as Ingenta, Intute, JSTOR, LION, Project MUSE or PubMed. Ask your tutor which one is the most appropriate for your subject. Alternatively, try looking on your department or library webpage. These often provide useful links to the best search engines. Look under 'study resources' or 'subject resources'. Most search engines allow you to search by key words, so that you can find material relevant to your project. You will be able to access some journals online, but for others you will have to actually go to the library and check out the journal. Some disciplines have one or two key journals that dominate debate. For example, in medicine *The Lancet* and the *BMJ* have very strong reputations, and are likely to get the pick of the best research. Find out which journals are most important for your discipline and keep an eye out for anything interesting there. If you are interested in further study in your area, this is a good habit to acquire. Look out for any interesting ideas for research projects or dissertation topics as you read.

Books

Many students are so reliant on online sources that they forget about the wealth of printed material in the library. In some science subjects you will not be encouraged to rely on book material, but for many academic disciplines the book is still seen as the most authoritative source for research. Your course guide may suggest some key texts for you to look at, but you need not stop at the end of this list. Aim to get a sense of what is in your library, and try out lots of different combinations of key words on your library computer to see what comes up.

The trouble with computer catalogues is that they often encourage you to look for one book at a time, find it and check it out, without stopping to browse. Books are usually shelved by subject, so the books nearby are likely to be dealing with similar topics. It can be tremendously useful to spend a few minutes looking along the book stacks to see if there is anything else relevant. Read the blurb on the cover, check the contents page and have a quick look at the introduction. These should give you a good idea if it might be useful or not. If you do find a particularly useful book, it is often worth looking in the bibliography at the back for ideas of more things to read. Your library probably has some of these books too.

Other disciplines

There is no law that says you have to stay in your own section of the library. Think creatively about the essay question you have been set. If you are studying politics, but your essay has an historical angle, you might want to look at something which will give you some background knowledge of the period. If you are writing about European history in the sixteenth century, you might want to read something about Reformation theology. If you are studying literature and you are working on a writer who has an interest in philosophy, art or religion, it can be useful to research the ideas that informed their work. A lot of critical books will tell you that Thomas Hardy was interested in the philosophy of Schopenhauer, but very few students bother to go and find out about him. Doing some extra leg-work in this way will give your essay a little more authority. But make sure that you remember the original focus of your essay, and do not ramble off into the other field.

Periodicals

Periodicals are magazines and journals published at regular intervals. The word is often used to describe contemporary scholarly journals, but in some disciplines it is used to refer to old magazines and newspapers. These texts offer a mine of good information about the past. In the eighteenth, nineteenth and early twentieth century, many periodicals carried articles about philosophy, science, politics, travel, architecture and fashion all side by side. You can also find contemporary reviews of books, plays and poems here. In centuries gone by, families often spent the evening reading periodicals aloud to each other, in the way that people nowadays sit down to watch the TV. This is therefore a rich cultural resource for any subject with an historical element. There are several online indexes that allow you to search for articles by subject, and many periodicals are available as online databases. Have a look on your library website or ask a librarian for some help.

Archive material

Your college or university may have an archive or special collections section. This may hold interesting rare books, printed pamphlets, records of local societies, letters, old lecture notes, manuscripts and a great deal more. This can be excellent material for you to explore, especially for a dissertation when you have a little more time on your hands. However, making use of this will require forward planning. The catalogue system may be different from the main library, so allow extra time to find things. Undergraduates and postgraduates can usually access archive material, although you may need special permission in the form of a letter from your tutor. Do not be afraid to ask. The chances are your tutor will be impressed and happy to help out. Your tutor will also be able to help you work out how to use this material effectively in your project. Working with this kind of source material can raise the standard of your research dramatically. It is also very interesting. Archivists are usually willing to offer help and advice to get you started.

Do not assume that all the good material is on campus. Your local civic library or city council probably has an archive. Your local newspaper will too. Many large companies and hospitals have archives and may be willing to let you have a look at their material for a relevant project. You will need to make an appointment to visit the archive, and you may need to give proof of your identity and take a letter from your university, so leave plenty of time to organize this.

Internet sources

There are many interesting and scholarly pieces of work on the internet. There is also a lot of superficial and inaccurate information. Be very careful about what you use from the internet. Sites which are sponsored by universities, academic publishers, academic societies or government departments are likely to give you very good information. Check the source of your information by looking at the second section of the url address. Think carefully before using and citing a source that includes **.com** or **.co.uk**. Unless you know this is a reliable source, choose something else. The following addresses are more likely to be reliable:

- **.ac.uk** – a UK university, college or school
- **.edu** – a US university, college or school
- **.org** – a professional organization or society
- **.gov** – a government or civil service department

Look on your department website for a list of useful and reliable links in your field. Be especially wary of study-notes sites, which may not bring your work up to the level that your tutors would like to see. Also, discussion boards and essays that are not published through a recognizable academic site often contain information which is simply not correct. There is nothing to stop you posting your work on the internet, so what you find through Google could just be the work of an enthusiastic undergraduate with some computing skills. Your marker will get twitchy if most of your bibliography is made up of internet sites. Make sure you use a mix of sources as you do your research. Reference internet material as carefully as you would reference printed material. Chapters 19 and 20 will show you how.

Ask yourself

- Do I have a mix of online and print sources?
- Where else could I look for some relevant material?
- Did I ask questions as I was reading?
- Are my notes accurate?

Learn to read

Effective reading is a complex skill and requires a lot of practice. As you explore your sources, think about how you can get the most out of them. Before you start on a text, think about the sort of things you are looking for to help your project along, but do not be so blinkered that you ignore other interesting elements when they crop up. Everyone has their own way of approaching a text, and for different assignments you will be looking for different things. However, here are a few strategies for reading.

- **Keep an open mind about the text.** One of the most valuable things you can learn as you study is the ability to suspend your own prejudices and preconceptions as you read. Learning to see things from different perspectives is a vital part of the reading process. Do not attempt to make a text fit your own agenda as you go along, or dismiss it because it challenges what you believe. You do not have to agree with the text, but give it a chance to speak for itself. If you react strongly to something, try to work out why.
- **Be critical.** This sounds like a contradiction of the previous point, but it is not. Critical thinking is more about asking

questions than forming judgements. So, as you read, ask yourself questions about the text. These will help you decide whether the text is sound or not. Ask the kind of questions a marker might ask about an essay. How accurate is it? Has the author missed something important? Have they used a useful method or approach? Did they apply it carefully? Have they come to a reasonable conclusion? Does the author seem to have a particular underlying agenda that may be clouding their judgement? Remember that a flawed text can be very useful when you are constructing an essay. So, if you find something you disagree with, do not put the text back on the bookshelf. You can use it in your essay and argue against it.

• **Think about language.** Keep one eye open for the language the author uses. This is especially important if you are studying literary texts. However, it is a useful way to read academic books and journals too. Look at the list of questions suggested for a close reading project on page 27. These simple questions give you an insight into the author's underlying concerns and preoccupations. Language does more than tell a story. It creates a world of ideas. So, do not just look at what the text says. Think about how it communicates with the reader. Doing this will sharpen up your writing too.

Taking notes

Some people like to take meticulous notes as they work through a text. Others prefer to read through swiftly and then return to look at the text in more depth. Develop your own style of reading and note-taking. However, here are a few things to remember.

• **Be selective.** Some students underline or highlight large sections of text, or copy out pages and pages of quoted material. This strategy can make you feel that you are working really hard and collecting lots of material. However, when you sit down to write your essay or dissertation you will have to sift through it all over again to look for a couple of sentences or a short phrase which you can actually use in your work. It is better if you can do some of the work of digesting your material while you are reading. Take notes from your reading in the same way that you would take lecture notes. Try to identify the main headings, the key ideas in each section or paragraph, useful examples and the overall argument. Any direct quotes that you note down should illustrate the main ideas. A few pithy phrases or sentences will be much more helpful later on than a photocopy of the article covered in bright yellow pen. Try to establish a balance between getting enough material and selecting what is really going to be useful. If you keep a note of page numbers, you can always go back for another look at the text if you really need to.

- **Note the page number.** This is obvious, but vital. Whenever you see something interesting, take a note of it and write down the relevant page number. This will save you hours trying to find it again later.

- **Note your references.** Make sure you have all the bibliographic information you need to reference the text properly. If you are unsure what information you should note down, Chapters 19 and 20 will help.

- **Keep your ideas separate.** Reading other people's work can often start a train of new ideas in your own mind, which you should write down quickly before they evaporate. Develop a strategy for keeping these ideas separate from the notes you are taking about the text you are reading. Otherwise, when you go back to use your notes to write up your essay or dissertation, you may be confused about who thought what.

- **Take care with quotes.** Make sure you get everything right when copying long quotes. It is very easy to get these slightly wrong or to miss out a word or sentence. Check the punctuation as well as the words. This can make a difference to the meaning. If possible, have the original text, rather than your notes, in front of you when you type a quotation into your essay. When proofreading your work, check your quotes against the originals if you can.

- **Be nice to library books.** Universities and colleges never have enough money for library books. Academic books are expensive to buy and can be difficult to replace if they are damaged or lost. Be gentle with your library books and resist the temptation to scribble on them as if they were your own. Somebody else will want to read them once you have finished with them. If you really want to mark pages or make comments in the text, use post-it notes or slips of paper.

Top tip

Use two colours of pen when taking notes on paper, or two colours of font on your laptop. Use one colour for your own comments and ideas and the other for anything you copy down word-for-word from the text, even short phrases. That way you will never get mixed up about what you need to reference. Alternatively, you could use a wide margin or brackets, or you could draw a box around your own comments.

Quick fix

- Leave yourself a realistic amount of time to find useful sources in the library and online. It may take a whole day to find what you need. This is an important part of studying. Consider this a good day's work, not a waste of time.
- Unless you have been told to, do not limit yourself to the recommended reading in the course guide. There are thousands of books and journals out there. Dozens of these will be of interest to you. Identifying resources is a key part of any project, so learn to use a range of sources. Think creatively about your question and keep looking until you find something useful.
- Be careful about what you use from the internet. Try to find reliable sites sponsored by universities and academic or professional societies. Avoid study-notes sites, online encyclopedias and independent webpages. Many of these contain flawed and inaccurate information.
- Take notes as you read and make sure that you write down page numbers, bibliographic information and url addresses. You will need these so that you can give accurate references to your work and so that you can find the material again if you want to check anything.

07

planning and structure

In this chapter you will learn:
- how to create a plan from your notes
- how to construct an argument.

Why bother planning?

Markers often complain about poorly structured essays, but by then it is too late to do anything about it. Bad structure in an essay is usually the result of a failure to read the question carefully, a lack of understanding of the subject, or a rushed job. Taking time to plan your work helps in many ways. It ensures that you connect your essay with the question. It reduces the stress of writing, as you know where you are going next. It produces a well-rounded piece of writing and a satisfying read for your marker. This chapter will give you some advice on how to construct a plan that fits your assignment. You will also find sample plans based on questions from Chapter 05 to show you some different models, which you could follow.

What sort of plan?

Whatever way you like to take notes and marshal your ideas, at some point you are going to need a linear plan for your essay. It is always worth doing this, especially in exams when time is tight and nerves are likely to make you forget a good idea or a useful piece of evidence. Remember what kind of essay you are writing. This is a good point to flick back to Chapters 03 and 04 and remind yourself of the shape of your assignment.

If you are writing a formal essay, you probably want to think about how your material fits the form of an introduction, a statement, a counterstatement, an analysis and a conclusion. If you are writing a project report, you will want to construct a plan that follows the model of abstract, aims of the project, methods used, results, discussion, conclusion. In some essays the plan is not quite so rigid. For example, a close reading can work through the set passage from beginning to end, or your question may ask you to look at certain themes or elements. In this case you should probably construct a plan with an introduction, a section for each theme and a conclusion. A case study could follow a formal essay pattern, or could work more like a project report. Be guided by your question and by the conventions of your subject. If you are in doubt, check with your tutor. Ask them to spend some time during a tutorial on this. The most important thing is to remember that you are not just making lists of what you know or what you have done. You are answering a question and the whole thing should form a logical argument with a clear outcome.

Sample plan for a close reading exercise

'Cock Crow'

Out of the wood of thoughts that grows by night
To be cut down by the sharp axe of light –
Out of the night, two cocks together crow,
Cleaving the darkness with a silver blow:
And bright before my eyes twin trumpeters stand,
Heralds of splendour, one at either hand,
Each facing each as in a coat of arms:
The milkers lace their boots up at the farms.

Edward Thomas

Write a 500-word critical analysis of Edward Thomas's poem 'Cock Crow' explaining the structure and argument of the poem, and commenting on such features as metre and rhyme, imagery and word choice.

Introduction: poem depicts moment of waking up at a farm

caught between night and day, opposites.

Metre and rhyme: formal structure

metre is roughly iambic pentametre,

most lines have ten syllables

but rhythm is sometimes interrupted, and internal rhyme disrupts pattern of poem, just as cockerels disrupt the quiet of night.

Imagery : reinforces theme of disruption and interruption

poem begins with image of felled trees

makes the reader uncertain where they are: 'wood of thoughts'

internal or external world? moment of waking

image of heralds seems out of place with farm life

ordinary milk maids, or something royal about them too?

Word choice: imagery supported by Thomas's use of language

'Cleaving the darkness with a silver blow' and 'Heralds of splendour' contrast with 'wood of thoughts' and 'the milkers lace their boots up'

use of rhyme also invites contrasts: 'night/light/bright' and 'coat of arms/farms'

double meaning of 'blow'.

Conclusion: this is a poem about contrasts and the splendour of ordinary things

these show both in form and language of poem.

(A completed version of this sample essay can be found in Chapter 08.)

....

A plan should operate as a skeleton for your essay. Ideally it should be possible for a reader to reconstruct your plan from the finished article. This is often what you are doing when you take lecture notes. Paying attention to how this process works will make planning your own written work a lot easier. Most lecturers think carefully about how they want to present material to the class. It might seem random, but if you listen, they will give you markers about what the main headings are and when they are filling out these sections. Look over your lecture notes and think about some of the techniques lecturers use. Try to see the shape of the lecture:

• Is the lecturer moving outward from a single text or problem to a wider context?
• Are they focusing in, beginning with background information, looking at a large cultural issue or scientific problem, and then exploring how one text or set of results contributes to this debate?
• Are they working through a text or an historical period in order?
• Are they offering a spectrum of different views on one issue?

These are all approaches you can use in structuring your written work. A clear plan makes it easier to fulfil your intentions.

Top tip

Keep your plan in front of you while you are writing. If you change your plan at any stage, write out a fresh copy so that you are absolutely clear about where your essay is going.

Look at the contents section of this book. The emboldened chapter headings are a tidy version of the plan I am using as I write. Ideally you want something that looks a bit like that, but shorter. You should also have a good idea of what goes in each section. I have chosen a plan that moves from general principles that you should think about before you start, through useful tools for planning to details about the finer points of language and referencing. The sequence is based on how you would go about constructing an essay from start to finish. But even with a clear plan, you will sometimes have information that could belong in more than one section. Do not be afraid to move things if they really seem to be in the wrong place. For example, Chapter 06 'Finding the right material' was originally intended to sit with the other chapters on source material in Part Four, but it made more sense to have this information earlier. If you find you are repeating yourself a lot, this may be a sign that you need to rethink your plan. Alternatively, you may change your mind about something, or find excellent new material as you work. You may need to alter your plan to accommodate this. Use your judgement about where things go and what belongs together. Your plan should be shaped by what you are trying to say. Try to give your essay direction, and keep thinking about the question.

....

Sample plan for a project report

Using a survey design, investigate whether optimistic bias among level-one students is influenced by socio-economic group.

Abstract: overview of the project

Introduction: what the project is about

explain optimistic bias: some people are unrealistically optimistic

Shephard *et al* (1996) applied this to student results

investigated why some students expect to do better than the average

but question of influence of social class still open

Aim: establish link between social class and optimistic bias in context of academic achievement

Materials and methods: how the project was carried out

participants and design: survey of 50 level-one students

equal gender balance (25–25) mix of subjects

procedure: explain how survey was carried out

20 questions about social background, parents' occupation, family income etc.

predicted marks of coursework, final degree, earning power after graduation

ten questions about sense of control over results

did students think their effort was a critical factor or not?

discuss statistical method used

Results: what was shown

report results of survey

lower-income group had lower optimistic bias (show chart 1)

gender did not make significant difference

but sense of control was a significant factor (show chart 2)

students from low-income group with high sense of control expect to do well

Discussion: put it in context

Sheppard (1996) showed that optimist bias varies at different levels of study

suggests that a range of factors are at work

Ruthig *et al.* (2007) and Kos and Clarke (2001) show that control is a key factor in determining optimistic bias

this supports our results

further work should look at ethnic group, private–public schooling, single-parent homes etc.

could also revisit same students to see what their results were at end of year

Conclusion: socio-economic group is a significant factor in levels of optimistic bias

but this can be counteracted by students' sense of control over their studies

References

....

Start writing

Once you have an outline plan, you can start writing. This can be the hardest moment of the whole essay-writing process. Everyone knows how intimidating a blank screen or page can be, but try not to freeze up at this point. Think of your plan as a map that will keep you on the right route as you navigate your way through your material. However, as with following a map, there is a point where you have to stop thinking about the journey, get your boots on and set off across country. Things often look rather different on the ground from how they look on the map, but that may not be a bad thing. Hopefully, your plan will have helped you to divide your material into several workable sections, which makes the task more manageable. The challenge at this stage is to put your material together in such a way as to form a coherent argument.

Many essay writers like to begin by writing their introduction, but there is no rule that says you have to start here. Introductions can be tricky. Often it is the fear of starting off on the wrong track or making some daft generalization which makes starting an essay seem impossible. If you have trouble getting going, it may help to forget the introduction for now and come back to it later. Even if you feel confident enough to write your introduction first, you may want to go back and rework the introduction once you have written the rest of the essay. In truth, an introduction has a lot in common with a conclusion. So, it is wise to make sure that they correspond with each other, and it may be easier to write them both once the body of the essay is complete. Chapter 09 has more advice on both introductions and conclusions. Many people prefer to start at the beginning of the main body of the essay and work forward from there.

Ask yourself

- Do I have the right kind of plan for my assignment?
- Does my plan move in a clear direction?
- Where are the weak points in my argument?
- Where will my evidence be most effective?

Creating an argument

The shape of the body of the essay will depend very much on the type of assignment you have and the topic you have chosen. However, every essay should try to present a logical progression which leads the reader through the material towards the key idea or conclusion. In a project report this is fairly straightforward, as the plan you should follow roughly maps out the process of your own investigation into the issue at stake. However, in other essays, you will have to create a route through the material you have studied in order to show why you have reached a certain conclusion.

Remember that an argument is more than a disagreement between two or more points of view. The argument of your essay is the line of reasoning which you use to make your point or explain your position. You are doing more than simply setting out facts and data. You are also giving reasons, explaining causes and drawing conclusions from these. You are showing why the evidence you have chosen supports your conclusion, and you are attempting to persuade the reader to your point of view.

To create a coherent argument you will need three key skills: selection, signposting and reasoning.

Selection

Make sure that everything in your essay connects to the question. Do not include data or information just because it is interesting, entertaining or took a long time to find. Try to work out which pieces of information or methodology are absolutely vital to your argument. What does your reader need to know before the rest of the essay makes sense? Put these elements in early on, and build up your argument from there. For later sections of the essay, choose examples and evidence that connect closely with these main ideas, and say why these are important or illustrative. Do not leave your marker to work this out on their own. They might assume that you did not quite understand the connection. Show that you understand what you are doing.

Signposting

This follows on from the previous point. Make it clear to your reader that you see how the different sections of your essay fit together. Demonstrate that you are building an argument by providing links between paragraphs and between different sections of the essay. Your introduction can help with this, but there should also be plenty of signposting within the body of the essay. You can refer forward to alert the reader to important material coming up. The end or the beginning of a paragraph is a good place for this. You can also refer the reader back to something that you mentioned previously which they should be bearing in mind. There is more about signposting and structuring paragraphs in the following chapter. That last sentence is one example of how it is done. Here are a few more:

Referring forward

'as the following example shows'
'the consequence of this action is'
'which will be demonstrated later in this study'
'evidence to support this idea includes'
'this issue raises a further question, which should be addressed'

Referring back

'as the previous example demonstrated'
'as has already been shown'
'in a similar mode'
'in contrast to the previous approach'
'using the method outlined on page 2'

Sometimes you can do the job of linking paragraphs with connective adverbs such as 'however', 'moreover' or 'nevertheless'. But use these words with care. They can be ambiguous if not used accurately. Show the reader exactly what connection you are making. Be as specific as you can, without sounding too pedantic, about how the different sections of your essay contribute to your argument. Try to avoid passive links such as 'which I mentioned earlier' or 'as I said before'. Make it clear why the earlier or later information matters now. Make sure that it does.

Reasoning

Try to keep a clear head and look at your topic in a logical, intelligent way. There is no quick way to learn this skill. Many colleges and universities have philosophy departments which offer courses in formal logic or critical thinking. This kind of course can certainly boost your powers of reasoning. However, you do not need to be a trained philosopher to write a well-reasoned essay. Move through your essay with a sense of purpose, and provide enough evidence and sensible argument to persuade your reader that your conclusion is valid. Avoid making jumps and quirky leaps between ideas, and make sure that one thing follows on from another. Test out your ideas as you go along by asking yourself difficult questions and looking for flaws in your own argument. Think critically about what you are saying as well as about what you read.

Sample plan for a formal essay

Critically appraise the potential of both quantitative and qualitative research methods in a rural social science topic.

Introduction: longstanding debate about relative merits of these approaches

and still an issue today (MacNeill quote)

define quantitative research = hard evidence, numerical, accurate, 'scientific', one 'truth'

but may be misread (Fielding quote?)

define qualitative research = discursive, interpretative, room for personal narratives and theoretical analysis, multiple 'truths'

but may be too vague or too narrow

this essay will focus on surveys and ethnographic methods as examples of data collection methods

Quantitative research: strengths and weaknesses

scientific methods, reliable, systematic, neutral/objective observer, like natural science

use McNeill and Chapman article and Usher

survey research = wide-ranging results, but sometimes data flawed needs statistical analysis and careful interpretation (Dale, 2006)

Qualitative research: strengths and weaknesses

very personal, subjective, allows multiple voices to be heard (Silverman, 2001)

social science different from natural science (Onwuegbuzie and Leech, 2005)

but ethnography sometimes seen as soft and subjective

researcher is involved in research process, but is always an outsider, barriers of language and culture

Attitudes of scholars: how do we decide what to use?

Purists = insist on one method

Pragmatists = happy to use a fusion of both

Situationalists = guided by nature of specific project

Conclusion: combining quantitative and qualitative methods can be successful

note examples of use of multiple methods (Cloke, Pawson, Giddens, etc.)

researchers should consider both methods

pragmatism is the best approach

....

Think critical

'Critical thinking' has become a key term in education recently, but most of the techniques of critical thinking have been around for a long time. This book has looked at many of them already. However, critical thinking is often used specifically as a name for the process of identifying strategies used to create and recognize logical arguments. This is a useful way of reading, as it helps you to see how a writer constructs a persuasive text – and where there may be flaws in their argument. It can also be a useful way of evaluating the effectiveness of your own writing. If you have studied logic at any point, many of the ideas in critical thinking will be familiar.

The key to critical thinking is understanding how an argument works. This is not quite the same thing as mapping out a plan to follow for your essay. An argument is an attempt to persuade. An essay should present a balanced argument. However, this overarching argument may contain two or more subsidiary arguments which interweave or contradict one another. So, it can be useful to think about the basic building blocks of one single argument. Most arguments contain the following elements: a premise, propositions, reasoning and a conclusion. See how these elements might fit into the following question.

....

With reference to recent reports, discuss whether local authorities should ban high-calorie, low-nutrition food in school meals.

- **Premise**: a starting point or assumption on which the argument is built. For example:

    School meals these days are less nutritious than those served 30 years ago.

- **Proposition(s):** a statement or statements which build up towards an idea. These statements are largely informational, but may be supported by evidence or examples. For example:

    1 Many schools serve burgers, chips and pizzas on a daily basis.
    2 Even in schools where healthy options are available, children are likely to choose high-calorie, low-vitamin meals.
    3 In recent years childhood health and behaviour problems have also increased.
    4 Schools which have banned unhealthy food report improvements in both the health and behaviour of children.

- **Reasoning**: a set of reasons and arguments showing how the propositions are connected to each other in order to show a chain of cause and effect. This may also incorporate evidence or examples in support of the reasons. For example:

    1 Although school meals may appear to be a small proportion of a child's diet, for many children, especially in low-income families, the school meal may be the most substantial meal of the day.
    2 As a result, many children are eating a low-nutrition diet.
    3 Recent medical studies underline the importance of diet for both physical and mental wellbeing.
    4 This suggests that the nutritional value of school meals is likely to have an impact on child health and behaviour.

5 Preventing child health and behaviour problems would save time, money and heartache for families, teachers and health authorities.

• **Conclusion:** a statement built on the preceding argument, which may contain a recommendation for further action or study. For example:

> Many health and behavioural problems could be solved by restricting children's access to unhealthy food. Therefore, local education authorities should consider banning deep-fried and high-calorie options at school meals.

The difference between a proposition and a reason is that a reason involves some element of cause or effect. It is not simply a statement of fact, but moves the reader in a certain direction, or appeals to a general principle. Reasons 1 and 2 show how school meals can have a high impact on a child's diet. Reasons 3 and 4 show that a connection between diet and behaviour may be more than coincidental. Reason 5 appeals to the principle that saving time, money and heartache is generally a good thing. A statement or set of statements cannot become an argument until it contains an element of cause or persuasion. The conclusion pulls together all the preceding points to assert the central idea of the argument.

To provide a balanced essay you might want to provide a counter-argument to this one, or to contest the validity of this argument. You can do this in several ways. For an argument to work, it needs to hold together as a whole. You can prove an argument invalid by showing that any of its sections do not work. The quickest way to savage an argument is to prove that the **premise** is wrong. In this case you would have to prove that school meals now are just as nutritious as they were 30 years ago. This would allow you to conclude that the rest of the argument was groundless and therefore not valid.

You could also challenge the **propositions** by showing that insufficient data had been gathered or that contradictory evidence existed. This would invalidate the reasoning which is built on the proposition statements. Alternatively, you could find fault with the line of **reasoning**. You could accept that school meals were low-nutrition but you could argue that there was not enough medical evidence to show a link with health and behaviour problems in the classroom. You could also argue that it was not the job of local education authorities to regulate children's diet. You could argue that this responsibility rests with families, who should teach children how to choose sensible food options. You could also argue that local authorities cannot afford the extra money to finance healthier eating in schools.

Finally, you could accept all of the arguments up to this point but draw a different **conclusion**. You could conclude that schools should stop serving meals altogether, thus making parents entirely responsible for their children's diet. Or you could recommend that no action be taken immediately, but that further studies and pilot programmes should be implemented to explore the matter further.

As you can see, there are many different points at which you could remove a vital part of the structure to make the argument collapse. But in order to do so convincingly you would have to present sound evidence and argument on the other side, which would in turn be open to scrutiny and attack. To write a strong, lively essay, you should present an argument in favour of banning fast food in schools, an argument against such a ban, and a section in which you weigh up which of the two arguments is the most convincing and why. Your essay should be a synthesis of these arguments into your own larger argument, which works to persuade the reader to your point of view. You should then offer a final conclusion and a recommendation, if appropriate.

Remember to apply the principles of critical thinking to the evidence that is used on both sides of the debate. For example, are there flaws in the medical or social studies and statistical data? Do they have false premises? Are they founded on representative samples of the population? Were they carried out over a long enough period of time? Did they overlook factors which could have had a bearing on the results? Do they use a methodology which is unreliable or outdated? Is their reasoning reasonable? Train yourself to ask these sorts of questions and to look for the strategies which scholars and writers use to convince you of their position. Critical thinking can help you see through weak and shoddy evidence. It will also help you construct strong, persuasive arguments of your own.

Quick fix

- Make a plan. Organize your material to fit the kind of assignment you have been set. If you reorganize your plan at any stage, write out a new version.

- Remember that your essay is an argument that should persuade the reader. Try to give it direction and purpose. Focus everything towards answering the question you have chosen. Work out at this stage which material you will use in each section.

- If you are writing a comparative essay on more than one subject, make sure you integrate them properly. Do not simply talk about one after the other. Explain the similarities and differences between them. Create a plan that allows you to bounce ideas between the two subjects and to build up a bigger picture.

- Think critically about your own argument and about the evidence you are using. Does this line of reasoning make sense? Is it based on unreliable information or on poor logic? Have you come to a reasonable conclusion?

08

sections and paragraphs

Links and breaks

Markers are hard to please. One week they will complain in the margin about work that is 'bitty' or 'choppy'; the next week they will complain about work that is 'soupy', 'too continuous', or if they have a rich vocabulary, 'ineluctable'. In both cases, what the marker has probably sensed is a problem with paragraphing. A good essay should strike a balance between creating a flowing argument and offering pauses and clear sections to the reader. A good essay needs both links and breaks. These are much more than window dressing. The links and breaks within an essay should reflect the underlying pattern of the argument. Handling these well allows your reader to see your essay plan in operation and to follow your argument clearly. This chapter will give you some advice on how to do this.

Subheadings

When you drew up the plan for your essay, you probably marked out several sections with subheadings. However, think twice before you type these into your essay in bold script. Some disciplines are very keen on subheadings and subsections within written work. Project reports in science subjects are likely to require subsections which are clearly titled. You may also be required to number your paragraphs, 1.1, 1.2, and so on. This ensures that your report is laid out clearly, that everything is in the correct section, and that your marker can find their way around swiftly. However, in arts and social science subjects, this may not be required. In fact, it may be seen as fussy and restrictive. A formal essay is the least likely piece of writing to require subheadings or numbered sections, as the point of this exercise is to create a continuous, coherent argument. Breaking a short essay up into subtitled sections can distract from the flow of your essay. Make sure you know what the standard practice is for your subject. If in doubt, check with your tutor.

Subheadings can, however, be very useful in longer pieces of work, such as honours dissertations. Any text over 5,000 words will probably read more easily if it has a few sections marked out. In a dissertation, subheadings will show your marker where you are going. They can also be very helpful to you as you write. They allow you to see whether one section of your dissertation has outgrown the others, and if another area of the project is rather thin. If this is a problem, you might want to consider revising your plan to accommodate your material, or splitting a large section in two. However, a few subheadings go a long way. Only mark major sections, and make sure that your heading really does reflect the content of the following section.

Whether you actually type out your subheadings or not, remember that you still want to keep your plan, with its sections and subdivisions, clear in your head. You also want to make it clear to your reader where those sections start and stop, and how they relate to each other. Your marker should be able to pinpoint where your introduction finishes, where the main body of the text begins, where the different sections within the body of the text fall, where this stops and where the conclusion begins.

Subheadings or no subheadings, the most impressive way to do this is through your language. The opening of a section should make it quite clear that you are moving on to deal with a new area of your topic, or to address a new perspective. Conversely, the end of a section should make it clear that you have said all that you have to say on the subject, and should perhaps offer a signpost for what comes next. This skill of signposting will keep your essay flowing forward, and will provide links between sections.

Paragraphs

Some students find paragraphing the hardest element of essay writing. This is partly because paragraphing practices vary enormously from text to text, and it can be hard to know which model to follow for an academic essay. Some markers have very strong opinions about the correct length and shape of paragraphs, while others do not seem to mind, and it can be hard to know whom to please. But really there is no mystique attached to paragraphs. A paragraph should be a group of sentences on the same subject. This paragraph is about the general nature of paragraphs. When I am ready to start talking about what you should do to write successful paragraphs, I will start a new one. Paragraphs do much more than provide a little rest for your reader every few lines. They are the building blocks out of which your essay is made. Each paragraph should express a single concept or idea. So, if you are having trouble sorting out where your paragraphs start and stop, it may be that you need to think a little harder in order to clarify your ideas.

Think about the plan that you have written for your essay. Think about the sections into which you have divided your argument. If you are writing a short piece of work, it may be appropriate to write a paragraph for each section. However, if you are writing a substantial essay or a dissertation you will probably have to subdivide each section into several paragraphs. Under your section headings you probably have a list of things you want to discuss or evidence you want to use. Allocate a paragraph to each one or, if you have a very complex idea in there, allocate a paragraph to each element of it. When your marker reads your work, they should, ideally, be able to recreate the structure of your essay plan from your paragraphs. Each paragraph should be a step forward in your argument. It should deal with one element of your essay or dissertation thoroughly and efficiently. It can help to think of each paragraph as a mini essay in which you introduce a new idea, present some evidence to back it up, and draw a conclusion from it. Once you have done this, start another one.

Like sections, paragraphs can be defined and linked by some careful signposting. You can link paragraphs together using connective words and phrases, such as 'however', 'consequently' and 'moreover'. Or you can use a longer phrase which links the material to something earlier or later in the section, as discussed in the previous chapter. Using a link to finish or start a paragraph makes it clear in which direction your essay is going. But try not to be too repetitive, and make sure that these links really justify their presence. There is no use saying, 'it follows that', if it is not obvious how one idea leads to the other. Sometimes there is no need to explain that one thing follows the other; sometimes it just does. If there is no need for a connecting word or phrase then leave it out.

Some phrases which look like signposts actually have no meaning or value at all. Avoid starting paragraphs with pompous declarations such as 'It is also the case that' or 'It is a useful observation to note that'. If you find any phrases like this in your work, cut them out. Your writing will be sharper and crisper without them. If possible, begin every paragraph with a strong statement. Avoid starting with hanging clauses. If you are not sure what these are, see Chapter 14. You should also avoid starting with vague pronouns such as 'it' and 'this'. If you cannot replace these pronouns with a real subject or noun, you might want to stop and ask yourself exactly what you are talking about. If you want to pick up an idea from the last paragraph and explore it further, that is fine. However, you need to name this idea clearly, to ensure that both you and your reader know what you are doing.

Top tip

Never use the same connective word or phrase twice in one paragraph. Words such as 'however', 'nevertheless' and 'despite this', signal a change of direction. Too many of these will make your essay seem rambling.

Markers are usually suspicious of paragraphs consisting of less than three sentences or rambling on for more than a page. Read through your essay once you have finished. If you find any paragraphs that are too long or too short, consider revising where the breaks fall. Do not use novels or newspapers as models for paragraphing. Novelists and journalists are not writing academic prose and are aiming for very different effects. Journalists rarely have more than one sentence in a paragraph, and often do not write complete sentences. They are playing a different game altogether, so you should not copy what they do. Here again, journal articles or academic books will offer good examples. So, pay attention to this as you do your research and learn to follow the standard practice for your own discipline.

Make the start of every paragraph obvious. Either you should leave an extra white space between paragraphs, in which case do not indent the start of your paragraph; or you should indent the start of every paragraph by hitting the tab key to the left of Q on the keyboard. This makes it very obvious where your paragraph starts. Be consistent about which system you use. Do not indent your first paragraph or a new paragraph after a subheading. Do not indent after a quotation, unless you are starting a new paragraph. For more advice on layout of quotes see Chapter 17.

Read the following essay, which is a short answer to the close-reading question planned out in the previous chapter. Look at the way in which the paragraphs follow the pattern mapped out in the plan on page 60. You should be able to identify the introduction, the three main sections and the conclusion. Notice how the opening sentence of each paragraph opens up the subject which that paragraph will discuss. If you were asked to give a summary of the essay in five sentences, you could use the opening lines of each paragraph and you would get a pretty good picture of what the essay is saying. Try to create strong opening sentences which have a little imagination, rather than simply saying, 'This section will discuss imagery' or 'Now I will turn to word choice.' Look also at the final sentence of each paragraph in this essay. These show that the paragraph is closing down, and clear the way for the following paragraph.

You should also look carefully at the introduction and the conclusion. They say very similar things, and deal with similar ideas, but they are phrased differently and emphasize different elements, so the conclusion does not sound like a repetition of the introduction. The introduction focuses on the cockerels crowing, which happens at the beginning of the poem. The conclusion deals with the milk maids, who are mentioned in the final line, so the essay gives the sense of following the movement of the poem, even though the central sections do not follow the order of the poem. There is more advice on introductions and conclusions in the following chapter.

Sample essay

Write a 500-word critical analysis of Edward Thomas's poem 'Cock Crow', explaining the structure and argument of the poem, and commenting on such features as metre and rhyme, imagery and word choice.

'Cock Crow' by Edward Thomas depicts an early-morning moment. Two cockerels crow in the darkness, rousing the speaker of the poem from sleep or wakeful thought. Thomas uses this moment to explore a range of contrasts: night and day, rich and poor, thought and reality. These contrasts are reinforced by Thomas's use of poetic structure and language.

This short poem has a formal structure of eight lines of iambic pentametre, but this rhythm is often disrupted. The first foot of the line is often reversed, as in the first line: 'Out of the wood of thoughts that grows by night.'[1] The trochee which falls on 'Out of' and which is repeated again in lines three, four, six and seven, interrupts the rhythm of the poem in the same way that the cockerels interrupt the quiet of night. Thomas's regular rhyming couplets are also interrupted by the internal rhymes such as 'grows', 'night', 'bright'. Thomas is clearly using the form of the poem to recreate the effect of disruption which is the subject of the poem.

The poem's imagery reinforces the themes of contrast and disruption. 'Cock Crow' opens with the image of felled trees within the mind, 'cut down by the sharp axe of light' (line 2). This internalized image makes the reader initially uncertain whether the action of the poem is within the mind of the speaker or external to him. Thomas thus recreates the effect of being woken from sleep or deep thought by sudden noise. The woods also locate the poem in a rural setting, which fits with the later references to 'milkers' and 'farms' (line 8). However, these images are contrasted with Thomas's conception of the cockerels as royal heralds, which seem out of place in the working world of the farmyard. The cockerels announce only the milkers, although this suggests that there is something noble and dignified about the role of these workers.

Thomas also creates contrast in his use of language. His use of rhyme sets up connections between the rhyming words 'night/light', 'grow/crow/blow' and 'arms/farms'. He also sets the heroic language of epic poetry against the ordinary language of the farmyard. In line four the cockerels are, 'Cleaving the darkness with a silver blow'. His use of 'blow', which carries the meaning of exhaling and striking, also connects the cockerels with his image of the felled trees. However, by the final line of the poem his language is everyday and mundane, as though with daybreak the speaker of the poem casts off thought and imagination and returns to the everyday working world.

Thomas's poem, through its use of form and language, invites the reader to juxtapose the final image of the milkers with the heroic richness of the epic world, and through this to recognize an element of splendour in even the most ordinary things.

(word count 489)

Bibliography

Keegan, Paul (ed.), *The Penguin Book of English Verse* (London: Penguin, 2000)

(This sample essay is referenced in MHRA style. See Chapter 20.)

[1] Edward Thomas, 'Cock Crow', *The Penguin Book of English Verse*, ed. by Paul Keegan (London: Penguin, 2000), p.843.

Quick fix

- Find out whether or not you are expected to have subheadings in your written work. Science-based essays usually require subheadings or numbered sections. Arts-based essays rarely do, except for long assignments such as dissertations.

- Use paragraphs to distinguish between separate ideas and to move your argument forward. Each paragraph should deal with one particular aspect of your essay. Use your plan to help you think about where the breaks should fall between paragraphs.

- Do not write paragraphs that are shorter than three sentences or longer than a page. Do not use novels, magazines or newspapers as models for paragraphing. If you want a model to follow, use academic books and journals in your own subject.

- Provide signposting links at the beginnings and endings of paragraphs. Make sure these links really earn their place. Take out any that do not actually contribute to the meaning of your essay. Avoid using a lot of connective words, such as 'however', 'moreover', 'furthermore' and 'nevertheless'. One or two of these in a paragraph will be fine, but too many can really slow your essay down.

09

introductions and conclusions

In this chapter you will learn:
- how to write strong introductions
- how to make conclusions conclude.

Beginning and endings

Introductions and conclusions can be difficult to write well, but they are not optional extras to your essay or dissertation. These are important sections, which are integral to the shape of your argument. Have one of each in every piece of work. The introduction and the conclusion should frame your work, making it clear and accessible to your reader, so it is important to get these sections right. However, many writers, even at very advanced levels, find constructing introductions and conclusions a challenge. So much seems to hang on these sections that they can appear very daunting. But do not worry. There are some strategies that you can learn which should help. This chapter will give you some ideas and advice.

There is an age-old maxim for formulating an essay plan, which goes like this: Say what you are going to say. Say it. Say what you have said. These three instructions equate roughly to your introduction, your main argument and your conclusion. This approach is fine up to a point, and certainly your introduction should flag up what your essay will be about, just as your conclusion should review and wrap up your material. However, and it is an important however, your introduction and conclusion should do much more than simply say what you are going to say and what you have said. Taking this approach too literally will leave you with a very flat and passive essay which seems to do nothing more than go round in a circle. What you really want are powerful, concise, interesting sections, which highlight the main themes and outcomes of your work. Both your introduction and your conclusion should provide an overview of your material, but the introduction should do so in a way that opens up the discussion or investigation, while the conclusion should do so in a way that provides some sort of closure.

Introducing introductions

An introduction should make it clear what the essay or dissertation is going to do. It should not be too loose. Do not use your introduction as a general dumping ground for background information that does not seem to fit anywhere else. Nor should you try to approach your topic in a wonderfully inventive, roundabout manner by spending three paragraphs talking about something else which is distantly but cleverly connected to your main idea. Try to zero in quickly on the area of your essay and to announce its main themes and methods.

On the other hand, your introduction should not be too narrow. Avoid repeating or rephrasing your question in the introduction. This gives the impression that in your reading and research you have not developed your ideas in any particular direction. It suggests that the essay which follows will be a rather mechanical, juiceless response to the question, rather than a lively, independent piece of writing. However, the introduction can be a good place to discuss the themes and problems raised by the question, or to focus in on the particular aspects of the issue which you plan to address.

Like the rest of your essay, your introduction should be specific, accurate and focused. This is not a good place to make grand, sweeping statements about the nature of your subject, or about themes and periods about which you know only a small amount. Do not make wild generalizations about 'public opinion', 'the Greeks', 'a number of biologists', 'all lawyers', 'middle-class people' or 'tradition'. Even in your introduction, you should demonstrate that what you are saying is reliable and precise. If you have a particularly quotable quote or a fascinating fact, your introduction may be a good place to show it off, especially if it raises some problem or dilemma that is central to the theme of your essay.

Do not begin your essay with a dictionary or internet definition of one or more of the terms in your question. This gives the impression that you had no idea what the question was about or where to start reading. An opening like this presents you as unsure of your subject and limited in your research. Also, the dictionary definition of the word may be slightly different from the specialized use of the term in your subject area, so this may not get you off to a good start. Nevertheless, defining your terms can be a good move early on in an essay or a dissertation. If you do want to begin in this way, it is much more impressive to find a discussion of the terminology of your subject in a scholarly book or article and start from there. Read some academic journal articles and see how other writers kick off. Try to assess which approaches are most successful and why.

The opening sentence can be the hardest one to construct. There seems to be so much to say all at once, that it is hard to know where to start. Remember that every paragraph should open with a strong, informative statement. Your opening paragraph is no exception. One of the best strategies I know is to limit the opening sentence of your introduction to no more than ten words. This forces you to say something interesting very concisely. It also makes your reader sit up and take notice. A crisp, short opening sentence will present you as a confident writer with a clear grasp of your material.

Passive and active introductions

Some introductions give the impression that the student is scared of the question and does not know what to do with it. Other introductions show that the student is in control of the subject and has an idea of how to tackle it. Try to create an active introduction that gives a sense of what you will do next. Imagine you are answering this question: **Explore the connection between marriage and money in Jane Austen's *Pride and Prejudice*.** A passive introduction would be something like this:

> Marriage and money are important themes in *Pride and Prejudice*. This essay explores the connection between marriage and money in Jane Austen's novel. First I will look at the theme of marriage, followed by the theme of money. Then I will look at the connection between the two. From this we will be able to see what Austen is trying to say about the link between them.

There is nothing really wrong with this, but it does not open up the question in an interesting way or provide anything to grab the reader's attention. A good introduction offers a sense of where the essay will go. Something like this is better:

> The connection between marriage and money lies at the heart of *Pride and Prejudice*. From the opening sentence to Elizabeth and Darcy's engagement, this novel highlights the desirability of financial security in marriage. However, this novel also shows the dangers of marrying purely for gain. This essay will explore the different models of marriage which Austen presents in *Pride and Prejudice*: marrying for money without love, marrying for love without money, and marrying with both. These models allow Austen to examine the place of the marriageable woman within the society of her period.

This introduction demonstrates knowledge of the text and some intelligent thought on the question. It also maps out the plan of the essay that is going to follow. If you can do this before you write the main body of the essay then your way ahead will be much clearer. However, it is always worth going back to look at your introduction once you have finished the essay. Does it promise something that is not in the essay? Or could you flag up an interesting idea in a more stylish way? Do not be afraid to rewrite the introduction if necessary. Think of the introduction as the shop window for your work. Show what you have in store in a way that will encourage someone to come in for a closer look.

Top tip

Reread your question before you write the conclusion. Make sure your conclusion answers the question.

Conclusions that conclude

Conclusions are also hard to handle gracefully, but it is better to try than to ignore the problem. As I have noted before, the easiest way to fail an assignment is to fail to answer the question. The easiest way to fail to answer the question is to avoid writing a conclusion, or to write a conclusion that is so hazy that your final verdict is not obvious. The one thing that a conclusion must do is to conclude. This is your last chance to make the point of your essay crystal clear. Use this opportunity well.

Some students worry that if they give a clear answer to the question they might reach the wrong conclusion and lose marks. However, you are much more likely to lose marks for having no conclusion than for coming to a flawed conclusion. Try to remember that your marker is testing more than your ability to state the correct answer. Your marker is also interested in your ability to use the methods central to your discipline and to argue well. Many essays, especially in arts and social science subjects do not have a 'correct' answer. It may be possible to reach a range of conclusions from the evidence available. Look back at the 'Think critical' section in Chapter 07 to see how a case could be made either way on one issue. What matters is that your essay as a whole builds up a case for the point that you want to make. If your essay has gone wrong earlier in the process, a vague conclusion will not help much. If your essay has built up evidence towards a particular point, then have the courage to drive this home in the conclusion. If the evidence is absolutely evenly weighted or is inconclusive, you can use the conclusion to discuss what would need to be done to provide a conclusive answer. But do not use this option as a get-out because you cannot be bothered to analyse or form an opinion about the material you have. Your marker will soon see through that approach. Use the conclusion to push your thinking towards some sort of resolution. Do not sit on the fence. Answer the question.

I've started, so I'll finish

Introductions and conclusions both sum up your essay and present its main point or points in a neat form. These two sections should correspond with one another to give the impression that your work is well-rounded and holds together as a piece. However, a well-rounded piece is not the same thing as a circular argument. Make sure that your conclusion is somehow a step further on than your introduction. Show that your thinking and your research have led you somewhere and that you have dealt with the problems and issues at stake. It can help to pick up a phrase or two from the introduction to create a link back to the start of the essay, but use this sparingly and make sure that you do something new with these repeated words and ideas. Otherwise your essay will seem to have travelled no distance at all.

Your conclusion can, of course, refer back to points you made earlier in the essay, but try to be brief about this. The conclusion is there to state your outcomes not to rework your material. Avoid introducing any new ideas or evidence in the conclusion, although a short, well-chosen quote may help to round things off. Do not save up your main idea as a punch-line. What you want to say should be clear from the start of your essay. Do not hold back a vital opinion, and do not attempt a clever 'twist in the tail'. The unexpected ending is great for detective novels, but not for academic essays.

Passive and active conclusions

Like introductions, conclusions can be weak and purposeless, or they can be active and full of energy. Here is an example of a passive conclusion, which follows on from the passive introduction on page 84:

> In this essay I have looked at the theme of marriage in *Pride and Prejudice* and how it connects to the theme of money. From this investigation we can see that Austen has complex

views about marriage and money. On the one hand she wants her heroines to marry well and have a secure future, but on the other hand she also believes that people should marry for love. There is a connection between the two because both marriage and money were important for people in Austen's time, which is why they are important themes in *Pride and Prejudice*.

This conclusion takes account of the fact that there is more than one way of approaching the issue of marriage and money in Austen's novel. However, it fails to offer a judgement about which one is of more significance. Pointing out the complexity of the situation does not offer any closure or resolution, although it could have been a useful way of opening up the issue in the introduction. The final sentence is a mirror image of the opening sentence of the introduction; it also has a strong flavour of the question. The essay in between these two sections may well have been interesting and well-informed, but the reader will put the essay down with the impression that this piece of work has not gone anywhere. Now consider this:

Austen clearly values love and emotional compatibility as elements of a successful marriage. However, the final pages of *Pride and Prejudice* demonstrate that Austen does not believe that a happy marriage is possible without the social and domestic stability which a secure income provides. Her subtle understanding of the part that money plays in sexual politics both before and after marriage is one of the hallmarks of her writing. W. H. Auden notes in his poem 'Letter to Lord Byron' (1937) that Jane Austen has a shrewd sense of 'the amorous effects of "brass"'. This unsentimental awareness is, as Auden suggests, the most 'shocking' thing about her.

This conclusion also takes account of both sides of the argument. However, it offers a much stronger statement about Austen's view of the place of money in marriage. The second sentence makes the message of the essay clear. The essay could reasonably stop here, but the final sentences provide a stronger finish. The third sentence connects the theme of the essay to a wider subject, in this case Austen's writing as a whole. This shows that the argument of the essay has an importance beyond its own boundaries. The reference to Auden's poem is not necessary, but it provides a little flair and shows that this student has read further on the subject than was strictly required. The essay closes on the strong idea that Austen's attitude to money within marriage is 'shocking'. The final statement provides closure, but it also leaves the reader with something interesting to think about. This conclusion keeps the essay alive and working hard right up to the last full stop.

Ask yourself

- What is the main idea in my essay?
- Are all the statements in my introduction accurate?
- Do my introduction and conclusion match the content of my essay?
- Does my conclusion answer the question?

Quick fix

- Use your introduction to outline where you are going in the essay. Avoid simply restating the question. Try to be interesting.
- Do not begin your essay with a vague generalization or a dictionary definition. Use well-researched, reliable sources from the very first sentence.
- Use your conclusion to point out how the evidence you have given answers the question. Push your point home and make sure you answer the question. Do not sit on the fence.
- Do not introduce new material or ideas in the conclusion, but do not repeat your introduction either. Find a new way to explain why what you have argued throughout the essay is important.

presentation

In this chapter you will learn:
- how to lay out your text
- how to present pictures, graphs and charts
- how to edit your text.

Looking good

You can lose the goodwill of your marker before they even start reading your work by presenting an essay or dissertation that is hard to read or poorly presented. Your work will be graded on how well it reads, but this can be helped or hindered by the visual layout of your script. This is equally important if you submit your essay electronically. Learning to create a tidy, readable text is a valuable skill in many areas of life and work, so it is worth practising this now. There are several things that you can do to make your script look good. These will not get you extra marks, but they might stop you losing some. They will put your marker in a better frame of mind, which is always a good thing.

- **Whose essay is this?** Make sure that you put your name, your course title and code, and your tutor's name clearly on the cover of your essay. The chances are that you will hand in your essay to a large administrative office where there may be dozens, even hundreds, of pieces of written work from a number of courses being processed at the same time. Make it obvious that this is your work. If your department or school requires you to fill out a cover sheet, make sure that you do this clearly and that it is firmly attached to your script. If you submit your work online or by email, make sure that your name, course title and code are included in the essay document itself, not just in the covering email.

- **Write the question at the top.** It might be obvious to you which question you are answering, but believe me, it is not always clear to the marker. Having the question on your essay also helps you keep the question in mind as you write. So, write the question at the top or on the cover of your essay. However, do not spend hours designing an elaborate title page. Your marker would rather see you put that time and effort into your written work. In exams there is no need to rewrite the question, but mark the number clearly both on your answer and on the front of the paper.

- **Double-space the text.** Many students are reluctant to double-space their text because it costs a few pence more to print out their work. However, your department may require you to double-space your work, and there are several good reasons why you should. Firstly, it makes the text easier to read. Bear in mind that your marker will be reading a lot of essay scripts and will get weary of looking at words and numbers. Anything you can do to keep your marker awake and happy is likely to work in your favour.

Secondly, if you do not double-space your text, your marker does not have enough space to mark corrections and comments on your work. Remember that essay feedback is a valuable tool for improving your writing. You want to encourage your marker to give as much feedback as possible. Leave space between the lines so that they can.

Finally, double-spacing text is standard practice in most areas of writing and scholarship, so it is a good habit to form. Although newspapers, books and articles are printed by publishers with single-spacing, all of these texts will have started life as double-spaced scripts. I am double-spacing my text as I write this book. This allows copy-editors and proofreaders to spot and correct any errors. If you go on to further study or to a job which involves producing texts of any sort, you will need to double-space your writing. So, start doing this now.

- **Leave a wide margin.** Leave white space on either side of your text. The default page set-up settings on your computer will probably be set at around 3cm. This should be adequate, but some departments have strict regulations about the width of margins. If this is the case in your department, then follow the rules that have been set. The reasons for a margin are the same as for double-spacing. You need to leave room for comments and corrections. These will be useful. Make sure you read them. For a dissertation or thesis that requires binding, leave an extra wide margin of 3.5cm on the left-hand side of each page. This will ensure that none of your text is lost in the gutter when the typescript is bound.

- **Use a sensible font.** Print your work in Times New Roman or Arial. These are the best fonts as they are easy to read and familiar to the eye. Do not imagine that a curly, cursive font will add class or style to your work. Your tutor will not be impressed. Use 12-point text unless directed otherwise. Anything smaller is hard to read. Anything bigger suggests that you might be trying to cover up for a short piece of work. Do not put quotations in italics, unless that is how they appear in the text you are quoting. Only use italics for titles of books and plays, or words in a foreign language. You can use bold text for subheadings and subtitles, but not for quotations, book titles or anything that you wish to emphasise in the text.

- **Give clear references.** This is easy when you know how. See Chapters 19 and 20.

- **Include a bibliography.** Even if you only have one or two texts to list, you should still give a bibliography or a reference list on the final page of your script. This is an integral part of your essay and will show your marker that you are recognizing the sources of your material. See pages 192–3 for advice on how to do this.

- **Include a word count.** Writing to length is a useful skill which you will need later on in life. Learn to tailor your work to the requested word length, and include a word count at the end or on the cover of your essay. If you are having trouble meeting the word limit, read through your essay with a very critical eye. Do you need all those big block quotations? Could you cut them down to a phrase or two instead? Is your writing full of little phrases that could be trimmed out, such as: 'it is worthwhile to note that' or 'it seems to be the case that'? Have you given too much detail, or not enough? If your essay is dramatically over or under the limit, you may need to go back and revise your plan for the essay. See the end of this chapter for some more advice about editing your essay.

If your essay is slightly over or under the limit, that is probably fine. Usually, you will not be penalized for an essay that is within 10 per cent of the stated word count, either over or under. However, you will be penalized for lying about it, so give an accurate word count. When marking essays for a whole class, it is usually easy for the marker to tell when something is too long or too short. Be honest about this or face the consequences.

Ask yourself

- Is my essay clearly marked with my name and course?
- Have I double-spaced my text?
- Have I explained my graphs and charts?
- Should I read through my essay one more time?

Pictures and maps

Use pictures and maps only where these are essential to your argument, not as decorations to make your essay look better. However, in some subjects, such as history of art or geography, you may need to include pictures and maps regularly. Make sure they are clearly labelled with headings such as Fig 1 and Fig 2. Make sure these numbers correspond to the numbers you use in your text to discuss the images. Write short, informative captions. Pictures, photographs and maps taken from published books and journals are source material, similar to quotations from text sources, so you should provide brief reference information in your caption and full information in your bibliography or reference list. See Chapters 19 and 20 for advice on referencing visual materials.

For photographs which have been taken to support your research, you should give a brief caption which explains the relevance of the picture and give the name of the photographer. If you took the picture yourself you do not need to say so.

If you have constructed a map as part of your research project, make it clear in the caption exactly what your map shows. For example: 'Excavated features of the Roman baths in Bearsden, Glasgow, showing the main phases of digging.' You should also say in your caption if you have based your map on a previous map. For example: 'based on Tithe Award map of 1837' or 'redrawn from Ordnance Survey map *Ballater and Glen Clova* 44 (2004)'.

Try to place your picture or map as close as possible to the text in which it is discussed. It is usually possible to insert a picture or chart into a Word document without too much trouble. If this is difficult for technical reasons, you can have an appendix at the end of your essay with all your visual material. Whichever way you do it, make sure everything is clearly labelled with Fig 1, Fig 2 and so on. Double check that the figure numbers in the text correspond to the correct figures in the appendix.

Top tip

Have maps, diagrams or other visual materials in front of you when you are writing about them. You will be less likely to get the numbers wrong or make a basic mistake.

Graphs, charts and diagrams

Graphs, charts and diagrams can be excellent ways of presenting material where you are dealing with a lot of numbers. Information which would seem bewildering when presented in text form can sometimes be more easily digested when presented visually. Underlying patterns can be seen more easily. Similarities and differences can appear more striking. If you have a lot of numerical information which you have gathered from a survey or from source material, consider constructing a graph or chart to help you present this.

There are many different forms of graph that you can use. What you choose will probably be determined by your material and by standard practice within your subject area. Look at a few journals for your subject and see how other scholars present their information. Keep the design of your graphs and charts as simple as possible. A basic chart or table with numbers in columns can hold a lot of information. See Table 4 in the example below. If you have good IT and design skills you could construct a pie chart or a bar graph to hold similar information. See Figure 1 in the example on page 96. However, it is more important to write a cogent essay than to produce a beautiful graph. Do not spend all your time on this.

....

Table 4 Proportion of each age group with a low income by area type

	Age band	Proportion in low income	SE
Remote rural	under 55	12.2%	1.2
	55–64	9.2%	2.1
	65–74	17.7%	3.2
	75 and over	26.7%	3.8
Accessible rural	under 55	7.1%	0.7
	55–64	6.3%	1.5
	65–74	14.9%	2.5
	75 and over	25.8%	3.6
Non-rural	under 55	11.0%	0.5
	55–64	9.8%	1.1
	65–74	12.4%	1.3
	75 and over	21.1%	1.8

Source: BHPS, 1999 wave.

Average income data provide no information about levels of poverty throughout the population. For example, it is known that income in rural areas is highly polarized, with a large number of individuals with a low income and a small number of comparatively wealthy individuals being typical. Identifying the proportion of the population with a low-income (defined as half median income) provides a more detailed picture of income by age group and by geographical area. Table 4 reports the proportion of each of the age groups by geographical area that fall into the low-income classification in 1999 (all differences are statistically significant). Regardless of area, those in the 55–64 age group are less likely than other age groups to be in the low income bracket. Thereafter, the likelihood of being in low income increases with each successive age band and, with the exception of the 55–64 age group, proportionately more of those living in remote rural areas fall into the low-income category.

(Philip and Gilbert, 2007, p.6)

....

The most important thing to remember when using graphs, charts and diagrams is that these are not substitutes for text. Your visual material is there to illustrate and support your text, but the text still needs to tell the story of your project and to analyse the numbers in order to build an argument. Do not leave the chart or graph to speak for itself. As with other types of information, graphs and charts are only as good as the conclusions that you draw from them.

Both Table 4 and Figure 1 are drawn from the same study about the income of older people in rural areas. In the short section of text adjacent to the table and graph, the authors have given a clear explanation of the type of material shown and how it is presented. They have drawn some conclusions which they will build on in order to develop their argument in later sections of this study. They have also cited the source of their numerical information. See pages 183 and 191 for advice on how to do this. Make sure that your visual material is accurate, carefully referenced and well integrated into your argument.

....

Figure 1 presents the income distribution by quintiles. It demonstrates that the incomes of the over 65s are more polarized than the incomes of younger age groups: regardless of location, older people's incomes are clustered in the bottom two quintiles. The proportion of those aged 65+ with an income that falls within the bottom 40% of the income range is lowest in accessible rural areas (63.5%) and the remote rural and non-rural areas are virtually identical at 68.6% and 68.2% respectively. The pattern for those with incomes in the bottom 20% of the distribution is different. Here the highest proportion, 37.8%, live in remote rural areas compared to 33.6% in accessible rural and 34.4% in non-rural areas. A possible explanation for this is that it is easier to access benefits advice in accessible and non-rural areas, resulting in larger numbers of older people claiming benefits which raise their income out of the lowest quintile.

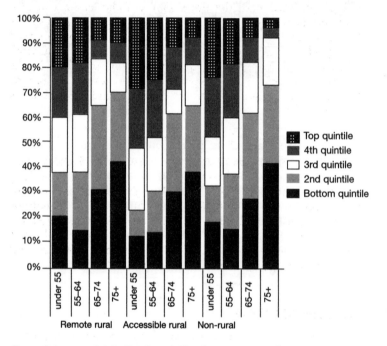

figure 1 income distribution by quintiles for area type and age group

Source: BHPS, 1999 wave.

(Philip and Gilbert 2007, p.6)

Reference list:

Philip, L. and Gilbert, A. (2007) 'Low Income Amongst the Older Population in Great Britain: A Rural/Non-rural Perspective on Income Levels and Dynamics.' *Regional Studies*, 41 (6), pp. 1–11.

(This extract is referenced using the author-date system. See Chapter 19.)

Equations

Leave a blank line above and below an equation. Use the tab key to indent from the left-hand margin or centre the equation:

$$x^2 + y^2 + z^2 = c^2t^2$$

Use the 'format font' function to create superscript numbers. Use italic script for variables such as x and y. This way x will not be confused with the times sign x. Italic letters will also stand out better when you discuss them in your text. Add spaces between numbers and symbols to make your equation read clearly. However, make sure you do not disrupt anything vital. Obtain Greek letters from the symbol font provided in the 'insert' function. If you have a run of several equations throughout your essay, use the tab keys to align the equals signs of each of them:

$$\xi^2 + \eta^2 + \zeta^2 = c^2\tau^2$$

Take care to make your equations readable and check your numbers and symbols carefully. If you must break a long equation in the middle of a line, place the split after a plus or minus sign, never in the middle of a term. If you use equations regularly you should learn how to use the equation editor function on your PC, which will allow you to create and insert more complex equations. Your department may have a helpful handout on laying out equations. Ask you tutor for advice.

Abbreviations

Abbreviations are a very handy way of compressing information – but only when both author and reader know what is being talked about, so use abbreviations sparingly. Too many in an essay can make the experience of reading the text rather like trying to decipher Morse code. However, the use of a few key abbreviations can help your essay to move forward more swiftly. Learn to observe the basic rules of using abbreviations and your work will be clearer and more accurate.

There are a few abbreviations which you can use without any explanation at all, for example: AIDS, BBC, DNA, IQ, NATO, UK, US. However, for the vast majority of abbreviations, you should not assume that your reader knows what your abbreviations mean. Write the title or definition in full on a first use. Give the abbreviated version of the title in brackets after the full title. Then you can use the abbreviated version without further explanation. For example:

Greenwich Mean Time (GMT)
Oxford English Dictionary (OED)
Scottish Chamber Orchestra (SCO)
United Nations (UN)

Abbreviations do not need full points (full stops), but initials in names do:

W. G. Grace
E. M. Forster
A. S. Byatt

Avoid pluralizing abbreviations if possible as this looks rather odd. However, if you cannot get around it, remember that you do not need an apostrophe. For example: ATMs, MPs, NGOs. This rule also applies to decades: the 1840s, the 1960s, the 70s, the 90s.

If you are working on a large project, such as a dissertation, which uses a lot of abbreviations, it can be helpful if you include a table at the beginning or end of your text, which maps out what all your abbreviations stand for. This provides a guide for the reader, who may forget the definition of an abbreviation between section one and section four of your essay.

Scientific abbreviations

In science subjects there are some abbreviations which are so regularly used that they do not need explanation. Here is a table of the most common ones. If you need to use these, make sure that you learn and apply them accurately. Note the difference between the upper- and lower-case letters in some instances.

ampere	A
base	b (as in kb)
candela	cd
Dalton	Da (as in kDa)
hour	h
kelvin	K
kilo	k
kilogram	kg

litre	l (US usage is L)
metre	m
millimolar	mM
minute	min
minimum	min.
mole	mol
molar	M (mole per litre)
second	s
Svedberg	S

Include a space between numbers and units, for example: 10 mM. Remember that none of these abbreviations ever takes s to make a plural.

Edit your work

Editing your work is a vital part of the writing process. When builders finish making a new house, the architect or project manager goes around checking that everything has been done correctly and neatly. When they find things that need tidying up or redoing, they create a 'snagging' list: a wobbly radiator, a door that does not open properly, a cracked piece of skirting board, a leaky tap. A good builder will come back to the house as many times as is necessary to get the job just right. A poor builder will say it does not matter, or it is not his job. He has done it once already and is not going to do it all over again. Think of editing your work as finding and fixing these 'snags'. Attention to detail and the willingness to work at getting things right are important and valuable skills. Learning to give this care and attention to your writing will also have spin-offs in other areas of your thought and action. Do not be embarrassed to be a bit of a perfectionist. High achievers are all perfectionists in one way or another.

This means that when you have finished writing your essay, you probably have not finished work on it. You need to check and correct what you have written. Even if you took meticulous care as you wrote, you will still find errors and things you could improve when you read your work through again. Do not try to do this as soon as you finish writing. Give yourself a break from the project. If you have time, leave your essay overnight and come back to it the following day. If you are in more of a rush to finish, take a short break and do something that will clear your head. Have a shower, go out for a walk, have something to eat or drink, phone up a friend for a chat or watch something on the TV for half an hour. Any of these will help you to come back to your essay with fresh eyes so that you can start looking for things you can brush up.

If you are writing a long piece of work, such as a dissertation, you should plan to leave yourself several days, or even a week or two, for editing and correcting your work. If you can rope in a friend or relative to help you with this, so much the better. It is always harder to find errors in your own work, because your brain expects to see the words on the page the way that you intended them in the first place. A second reader will pick up more typos and slips of grammar than you will. However, they should not change or comment on the content of your essay (see page 172).

You will always pick up more errors if you print out a draft copy to correct by hand. Your essay will look a little different on paper from the way it does on the screen, so this can help you to spot mistakes. You will also see if there are problems with formatting, page breaks, or footnotes. Remember to check numbers as well as words. Your eye will not be drawn to wrong numbers as it will be to wrong letters, so double check that any numbers are absolutely correct.

If you are naturally a quick reader, take extra care. Quick readers often acquire their speed through the ability to recognize whole phrases on the page in a single glance. Such readers are particularly prone to skipping over small errors such as two letters the wrong way round in a word, or a double 'the', or an 'it' instead of an 'if'. If you are a quick reader, then slow down for this task. Read the essay at the speed at which you would read it out loud. Make sure the text really does say what you think it does.

The next part of this book will give you some detailed advice on the sort of issues which you should think about while you are editing your work. However, try to think of good grammar, punctuation and spelling as important elements of your writing, not just as last-minute glitches to correct. Learning to use language correctly will help you present your ideas well. Show your marker that you care about producing a carefully constructed, neatly presented, error-free text. They will be impressed.

Quick fix

- Make sure your essay is clearly marked with your name, your tutor's name, course code and title. You cannot get the marks for your essay if nobody knows who wrote it.
- Present a readable and markable script. Follow department guidelines about spacing of text, fonts and margins. This will help to leave room for your marker to write in valuable feedback about your essay.
- Lay out visual material with clear captions and references. Explain the significance of any graphs and charts in your text. Do not leave the numbers to speak for themselves.
- Write abbreviations out in full the first time you use them. If you have a lot of abbreviations in a long piece of work, provide a list of abbreviations.
- Take time to edit your work carefully. Print out a paper copy and edit it by hand. You will spot many more errors than if you read it again on the screen.

Try it out: Building your answer

What is wrong with the reasoning in the following extracts?

1 Hamlet's indecision leads to his own tragic death and the death of innocent bystanders such as Polonius, Ophelia and Laertes. Therefore, Shakespeare's play shows that indecision is the cause of tragedy. Hamlet should have killed Claudius sooner.

2 Because primary-school children are naturally reluctant to learn, teachers need to develop strategies to engage their attention and encourage effort in the classroom.

3 Poor essays often contain many surface errors. Students who read quickly are prone to missing surface errors when they check their work. Therefore, students who read quickly generally write poor essays.

4 In the 1840s and 50s many miles of railway track were built and more people began to travel by train. In these decades, sales of fiction also rose dramatically. From this it is possible to deduce that sales of fiction increased because many people were buying novels to read on long train journeys.

Editing your work: Find the surface errors in the following extracts.

1 If excercise cannot prevent coronary heart disease (CHD), one must ask whether excercise can lessen the risk of CDH. The point that must be borne in mind is that psychical activity is only one possible primary preventive measure, other preventive measures include taking up smoking, lowering blood pressure and a lowering of serum total cholestrol.

2 Since independance, Kenya has insured a rapid expansion in the numbers of traders and beureaucrats by a process of legislation and licencing: e.g. the Trades Licencing Act of 1867. The government also saw to it that the fertile 'White Highlands' were distributed among settlements in schemes such as the Million acres Scheme. The point behind such provision was capitalist in principal.

3 Hamlet is a a famously complex play. Complex and difficult to understand in the sense that at the end of the tragedy many questions are left answered. Hamlet is not a typical tragic hero. (Although it is important to remember that the character of Hamelt can be interpreted in many different ways.)

4 Mixing quantative and qualitative methods provide more valid and reliable results, there are two fundamental questions to be asked by the researcher when considering using the mixed method, firstly, what is the most suitable data collection method for the data to be collected, and secondary, how can the data be most effectively combines or integrated?

Answers can be found on pages 199–201.

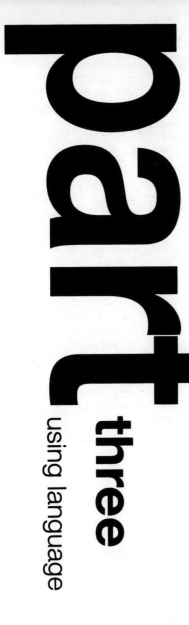

part three

using language

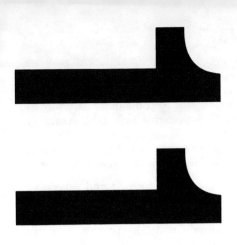

11

academic style

In this chapter you will learn:
- how to make language work for you
- how to get the tone of voice right for your essay.

Writing with style

Your research may be thorough and your argument may be brilliant, but your essay is never going to excel unless you are able to express yourself well. For this you need a good command of language. Using language well seems to come quite naturally to some people, while others find that this skill takes years to acquire. Whatever your language skills are now, there will always be ways in which you can improve your use of English, or find more stylish and accurate means by which to make your point.

The following chapters will give some focused and accessible advice on writing for academic work. Most of the pointers here are to do with punctuation, common grammatical errors and spelling, and will connect closely with the process of essay writing. This part of the book is not intended as a comprehensive course in English language and grammar. If you feel you need more advice or support in this area, you could try looking at *Teach Yourself Correct English* by B. A. Phythian and Albert Rowe. Alternatively, see the end of this book for some more ideas on further reading.

If your grasp of English is generally fine, but you would like to sharpen up your understanding and use of the language, there are two good ways to do this. One is to learn a second language. If you have never studied another language, you may never have thought about how language works or about the rules of grammar that hold each language together. An evening class in French or Italian not only gives you access to a whole other experience of using language; it will also help you make sense of how English operates.

Another good way to improve your writing is to raise the stakes in your own leisure reading. Steer clear of thrillers and romantic fiction for six months, and invest in a few classic novels. Jane Austen, Charles Dickens, Robert Louis Stevenson, Elizabeth Gaskell, Thomas Hardy, Joseph Conrad, Virginia Woolf, F. Scott Fitzgerald, Ernest Hemingway, John Steinbeck, Graham Greene – the list goes on. All of these writers are masters of using language to communicate. In dramatically different ways, they can make words do almost anything. Immersing yourself in prose of this quality is bound to rub off sooner or later. Remember that you do not necessarily want to copy any of these styles of writing. You want to get a sense of the underlying patterns of language, and to develop an ear for what sounds good and what does not. You might as well learn from the best.

However, there are a few specific rules and conventions of academic language, and you will need to learn these at some point. Tutors rarely give this advice out in class, although when marking they are quick to correct mistakes in this area. Students sometimes feel that they are expected to know these rules by magic. Often the only way to learn about academic style is to put together information piece by piece from the comments in the margins of your essays. This process can take a long time – which is, I suspect, why many students struggle with written work in the early stages of their degree, and then suddenly flourish in their final year. The following sections should help, but if you do receive any advice on this issue from your tutors and markers, try to take account of it. Developing a confident academic style in your writing will give your work weight and authority.

Register

Writing well involves presenting your material in a tone appropriate to your audience and to the task in hand. Think about the many different styles of written language which you might read in a single day. You could encounter different registers of language in a business letter, a newspaper report, a text from a friend or a short story. Each of these styles might do its job well, but they would all be distinct from the others, and none of these registers would be quite the right thing for your essay. Spoken language is different all over again. Not many people talk in neat, grammatical sentences. So, do not try to put your thoughts down on paper exactly as you would relate them to a friend if you were speaking out loud. You need to develop a suitable 'tone of voice' for your written work. An academic essay is a formal document and requires a formal register, but this does not mean that it needs to be posh, long-winded or full of jargon.

Students often struggle to find a balance between formal, intellectual language and open, accessible English. Many professional scholars struggle with this too, which is why some academic books are so hard to understand. However, even the most complicated ideas can be articulated clearly. Einstein's first Relativity paper 'On the Electrodynamics of Moving Bodies' (1905) begins by explaining why time must be a relative concept, through a simple prose description of moving trains and flashing lights. Watson and Crick's groundbreaking 'Letter to *Nature*' (1953), which revealed the double-helix structure of

DNA, is also a model of clear, concise writing on a sophisticated topic. The letter takes up one page, but all the essential information is there, and it can be followed by a reader with little specialist knowledge. Being able to explain an idea simply is often a sign that somebody really understands what they are talking about. Your marker will be delighted to see complex ideas presented in plain English. They will also notice if you dress up weak thinking in flowery language. So, pay attention to the register of your writing and remember who will read your work.

Read academic texts

The best models for you to copy for your academic work are the articles and books written by scholars and researchers in your subject area. This is handy for you because you need to read these texts anyway for your own research. So, as you read articles and secondary sources try to look at the ways in which other scholars and writers use language. If these seem too dense and formal then do not copy their style. However, if you find a book that is lucid, interesting and readable, try to work out what makes it so accessible. Think about:

- the length of the sentences
- the kinds of words that are used
- how much technical language is used.

In academic writing you want to strike a balance between complexity and simplicity. On the one hand you should sound intelligent and well-informed; on the other hand you should be clear and comprehensible.

Is 'I' too personal?

Your name appears on the front of your essay, therefore your marker already knows that everything in the essay is your opinion. Do not keep saying 'in my opinion' or 'it seems to me that'. Have the courage of your convictions and state what you think. If you can back up your views with evidence from your research or from primary or secondary sources, there is no need to apologize or hesitate.

Some markers dislike the use of 'I' anywhere in an essay or dissertation. However, the trend in academic writing is moving toward accepting it, especially in science. For project reports where you are recounting what you and your classmates did in the lab, it probably makes sense to use 'I' and 'we'. The same applies to learning logs, where your learning experience is the subject being studied. For an essay about the French Revolution, where you may be analysing the causes of events over 200 years before you were born, it is probably better to avoid talking about yourself.

Whether you use 'I' or not, remember that your essay is a formal document. The marker does not want to know about the disagreement you had with another student in the project team, or that you were depressed during your placement because you had just broken up with a boyfriend or girlfriend. Present your work as a piece of cohesive thought and research rather than as a collection of your own responses. Your tutors are trying to train you to be objective and analytical, so demonstrate that you are developing these skills.

Avoid slang

This does not just cover words and phrases. You also want to steer clear of informal expressions and sentence constructions. Avoid saying things like: 'This picture really hits you between the eyes when you see it.' You can express much the same thing by saying, 'This is a picture of enormous emotional power,' or, 'This picture demands a strong emotional response.' As with 'I', it is best to avoid using 'you' or 'us' for the reader of the text. 'One' usually sounds rather formal in everyday speech, but it can be very useful in this setting. For example, you could say, 'This picture appeals strongly to one's senses and emotions.' Remember that you are not just writing down your usual, everyday speech. Have the confidence to use a correct, academic style.

Top tip

Txt spk is ok for ur m8s, but try not 2 let any sho up in ur SA. Lrn 2 rite propr 4mal nglish.

Avoid being too clever

Some of the worst grammatical errors in essays are caused by students trying to write long, complex sentences. Remember that crisp, simple language was good enough for Einstein and for Watson and Crick, so it should be good enough for you too. Use the technical language of your subject where it is appropriate, but do not try to glamorize your essay by making it sound 'intellectual'. Always use the shortest possible sentence for what you want to say. Similarly, do not use words that you think you understand. If you have the slightest doubt about a word, look it up or leave it out.

Tenses

Tenses are all about when things happen. Something may happen in the present in which case it goes in the present tense: **is, has, says, argues.** Or it may have happened in the past, in which case it goes in the past tense: **was, had, said, argued.** When writing academic essays you should use the past tense to describe historical events or to recount an experiment, project or placement in which you were involved. However, when you are talking about research that you have read, you should normally use the present tense to describe the views of other scholars and researchers. For example:

> Justin Kaplan **notes** that, John Jacob Astor **was** the richest man in the United States when he **died** in 1848. Kaplan also **claims** that Astor **was** 'the young nation's first millionaire' (2006, p.13).

However, if you are contrasting old scholarship with new scholarship you could discuss the old scholarship in the past tense and the new scholarship in the present tense to emphasize the difference.

If you are writing about literary texts, the same guidelines apply. Use the present tense for anything that happens in the story, novel, play or poem that you are discussing. Use the past tense for historical events or events in the life of the writer. This helps to keep the fictional world and the real world separate:

> Henry James **was** an American novelist who **lived** and **wrote** in Europe. In *The Portrait of a Lady* he **explores** the social tensions which **surround** Isabel Archer as she **moves** between these two continents.

Avoid contractions

Contractions are shortened words, with an apostrophe, which have been made out of two words squashed together. These include **isn't, couldn't, would've, that's, it's, you're, they're.** In an academic essay you should write these out in full. So, **isn't** becomes **is not; couldn't** becomes **could not; would've** becomes **would have; that's** becomes **that is; it's** becomes **it is; you're** becomes **your are; they're** becomes **they are,** so on.

There are three good reasons for writing these contractions out in full. One is that it sounds better. Removing the contractions is one of the quickest ways of making your essay sound less chatty and more formal. The second reason is that some of these contracted words are often confused with other words which sound like them, such as **its, your, there** and **their.** Writing the contractions out in full means that you are less likely to get mixed up about which word you want. Finally, many people have trouble handling apostrophes, so make life easy for yourself by only using apostrophes where you really need them. There is some more on this issue in the following chapter.

Ask yourself

- Does my essay sound like I know what I am talking about?
- Which academic text was easiest to read when studying for this essay?
- What is my bedtime reading these days?
- Do I know the difference between **it's** and **its**?

Quick fix

- Write in clear, simple, formal English.
- When you read academic texts, keep one eye open for the kind of language and tone writers in your discipline use. Do not attempt to copy the style of anything that is complex or hard to understand. Look at the books and journals that you find straightforward and helpful. Learn to write like this.
- You can use 'I' in an essay where it is appropriate. For a project report or a learning log this should be acceptable. However, you should still try to sound objective and analytical.
- Write about historical events in the past tense. Write about scholarship, fictional characters and fictional events in the present tense.
- Do not use contractions in your essay. Write words out in full.

12 punctuation matters

In this chapter you will learn:
- where to put apostrophes
- how to use commas effectively.

Who needs punctuation?

Punctuation matters. It does not simply tell the reader when to start and stop; it organizes the text into meaningful units, and shows the relationships between these units. Getting it wrong can seriously damage the sense of the text. If you do not believe that punctuation makes a difference, look at this example which is quoted in Lynne Truss's book, *Eats, Shoots and Leaves: The Zero Tolerance Approach to Punctuation* (2006, p.9).

Dear Jack,

I want a man who knows what love is all about. You are generous, kind, thoughtful. People who are not like you admit to being useless and inferior. You have ruined me for other men. I yearn for you. I have no feelings whatsoever when we're apart. I can be forever happy – will you let me be yours?

Jill

Dear Jack.

I want a man who knows what love is. All about you are generous, kind, thoughtful people, who are not like you. Admit to being useless and inferior. You have ruined me. For other men I yearn! For you I have no feelings whatsoever. When we're apart I can be forever happy. Will you let me be?

Yours, Jill

It makes you think, doesn't it?

Apostrophes

The misuse of apostrophes is one of the most common problems in written English. One can see apostrophes in the wrong places in shops, theatre programmes, adverts, newspapers, restaurant menus and more. There is always some public debate going on about whether we should retain apostrophes in the language or abolish them because so few people seem capable of using them properly. However, the fact is that they still exist, and your tutors still expect you to be able to put them in the right places. Before writing this book, I asked my colleagues what they thought was the biggest problem in students' written work. Wrong use of apostrophes was overwhelmingly at the top of the list. The reason this annoys markers so much is that the rules are pretty simple. Here they are.

You can use an apostrophe to:

- **signal possession by adding 's to a singular noun: Susan's** book, **King's** College, the **boy's** father, the **woman's** coat, the **banana's** skin.

  If the noun or name already ends in s then go ahead and add 's as normal: **Tess's** book, **Dickens's** novels, the **bus's** driver.

  A plural noun ending in s takes an apostrophe after the s: the **boys'** fathers, the **ladies'** toilet, the **horses'** owner.

  A plural noun not ending in s takes 's: the **women's** rights, the **children's** school.

  Get into the habit of taking a moment to check if the apostrophe should be before or after the s every time you use one. Do not tuck the apostrophe into a name that already has an s: **Dicken's** novels, **Jame's** coat. Similarly, do not tuck an apostrophe into possessive pronouns (see below).

- **signal a missing letter in a contraction such as don't, won't, isn't, it's.** However, as I mentioned in the previous chapter, these contractions are informal and should not appear in academic essays, except when they appear in quotations from texts. Write out these phrases in full: **do not, will not, is not, it is.**

Do not use an apostrophe for:

- Plurals of nouns ending in vowels such as **banana's, piano's, tomato's** instead of **bananas, pianos, tomatoes.** This is known as the 'greengrocer's apostrophe', but it crops up everywhere. There is no excuse for this; it is just plain wrong.
- Possessive pronouns such as **hers, yours, theirs, its, ours.** These are complete words, like **his** and **mine.**

It's and **its** are commonly confused, but this really annoys your marker, so get this one right. **It's** should never appear in your written work. If you mean **it is**, then write this out in full. If you mean belonging to it, then there is no apostrophe. Also look out for **who's** and **whose.**

Top tip

Once you have written your essay, use the 'find' function to run a search on your essay for **it's.** Go through these one by one and correct them to **its** or **it is.**

Commas

I used to be a sub-editor on a daily newspaper. I would get a rough and ready news story from a reporter, and I would cut and correct it. I would put their commas in the right places. I would send it to the chief sub-editor who would look over it and put my commas in the right places. He would send it to the night editor, who would approve it, and put all *his* commas in the right places. We all thought we were correct.

Different writers vary in their use of commas, which can be confusing when you are getting to grips with the rules. In the last 40 years, English has shifted quite radically to using as few commas as possible. Someone who went to school and university in the 1960s will have learned different rules from accepted contemporary practice. However, this does not mean that you can put commas wherever you like. Commas provide the internal structure of each sentence. They mark out which bits of the sentence are essential to its meaning and which bits are supplementary. They show where clauses start and stop, and they separate items in lists. Getting them in the right place keeps the movement of the sentence clear, but having too many can slow down your reader and make the sentence seem cluttered. Here are some rules which you should learn to observe.

You can use a comma:

- **to link two sentences with a conjunction (and, but, because, or).** This makes a compound sentence. There is a clear example of this kind of sentence in the opening paragraph of this section. The second sentence could be split into two:

  ✓ I would get a rough and ready news story from a reporter. I would cut and correct it.

I have chosen to link the two sentences with a comma and the word **and** to emphasize that I want the reader to take both sections as part of the same event. However, a comma cannot link two sentences by itself. If I insert a comma but miss out the word **and**, I create a comma splice (see below). Technically it is possible to link together several sentences with commas and conjuctions to make a very long, complex sentence. Novelists such as Virginia Woolf and Henry James do this all the time in their fiction, but you should avoid it. Limit yourself to one conjunction per sentence where possible. In essays, it is always better to write short, clear sentences.

• **after connective adverbs.** These words can be useful at the beginning of sentences in essays as they show how your argument is moving from sentence to sentence. **However, yet, still, nevertheless, therefore, thus, moreover, for example** and similar words are used to suggest a connection or contrast between two sentences without formally joining them. A comma is required after one of these when it appears at the beginning of a sentence.

✓ However, you will always make occasional mistakes.

However is particularly problematic. If you leave out this comma, it sounds like the whole sentence is a subordinate clause which should lead to some other statement. If **however** is operating as part of a subordinate clause, the comma goes after the clause:

✓ However much you try, you will always make occasional mistakes.

This is easy to get wrong, so look out for this one. There is more about clauses in the following chapter.

Though and **although** cannot be used as connective adverbs at the start of sentences:

✗ Although, many people try to do so.

They can, however, be used at the start of a subordinate clause:

✓ Although Elizabeth finds Darcy overbearing, she is obviously the only woman in the novel who is his intellectual equal.

• **to separate items in a list.** This works for nouns and adjectives:

✓ Oscar Wilde wrote novels, plays, poetry, journalism, criticism and children's stories. However, he is most famous for his colourful, controversial and self-destructive private life.

If you have three or more items, you should use **and** between the last two. Avoid listing verbs and adverbs. One at a time is quite enough.

• **to signal parenthesis.** Commas can be used like brackets to insert an extra piece of information, interesting or otherwise, into a sentence. Reread that last sentence without the words between the two commas. It still makes sense. The phrase between the commas is not a complete sentence. In this case it is a modifying phrase, which adds some extra information or comment about the preceding noun. The first comma signals a short diversion from the sentence. The second comma shows that this diversion is finished, and the sentence picks up where it left off. You could insert a different phrase or clause here, such as 'or even a witty aside' or 'if you have any extra information to insert'. Parentheses have great comic potential, but try to resist the temptation to use them in essays for hilarious remarks that probably will not seem so funny to your marker. Also avoid using them to include lists of things that you would like to mention but cannot be bothered to include properly in a working sentence:

✗ Hamlet has many flaws, indecisiveness, arrogance, suspicion of others etc., which undermine his heroic potential.

Here it would be better to say:

✓ Hamlet has many flaws which undermine his heroic potential. He is indecisive, arrogant and suspicious of others.

It sounds less muddled. Also, avoid long, rambling diversions in sentences, or diversions within a diversion. One short phrase is fine, but if your parenthesis is any longer than eight words, you should consider putting this information in a sentence of its own. If you do use commas to form a parenthesis, make sure you close it. You would not use just one bracket. In fact, avoid brackets and dashes wherever possible. Good use of commas is much more elegant.

- **to mark out clauses.** If you are hazy about what a clause is, you need to read something that will explain the basics of grammar slowly and carefully. Try *Teach Yourself English Grammar* by Ron Simpson. Traditional grammar marks every shift in the syntax of a sentence by inserting a comma. Modern writing is more relaxed about this. Look at sentences four and five in the opening paragraph about commas on page 115. These sentences are grammatically identical, but I have only put commas in one of them so that you can see the two styles in action. Aptly enough, the chief sub-editor liked to take commas out whenever possible, while the night editor liked to put them back in. In that particular case it does not make much difference. The syntax, or sense, of the sentence works either way.

Some clauses do not need to be separated by commas, especially when a linking word, such as **that, whenever** or **since,** is used to signal a relative clause. However, commas can make a dramatic difference to the meaning of this kind of sentence. Leaving them out can make a sentence ambiguous. You will find an explanation of relative clauses on page 133, which should help you understand how this works. Use commas to make your meaning apparent, not just to provide pauses where you think the reader needs a rest. The easiest way to get this right is to be absolutely clear in your own head about what you want to say, and to say it as simply as possible in short sentences.

• **to introduce speech.** A comma is used to introduce speech or a quotation when it forms part of the preceding or following sentence:

✓ Hamlet says, 'I know a hawk from a handsaw.'

or

✓ 'I know a hawk from a handsaw,' says Hamlet.

You can also use a colon to introduce a quotation or speech:

✓ Hamlet says: 'I know a hawk from a handsaw.'

Always use a colon when the quotation follows a complete sentence:

✓ Hamlet insists that he is sane: 'I know a hawk from a handsaw.'

Do not use a comma:

• **to join sentences without a conjunction.** This creates a comma splice, which is next to dodgy apostrophes on the marker's hate-list. A comma splice looks like this:

✗ Some markers are sent into a rage by comma splices, they will give themselves a hernia with fury, and will cover your essay in red pen.

It should read:

✓ Some markers are sent into a rage by comma splices. They will give themselves a hernia with fury, and will cover your essay in red pen.

✓ Some markers are sent into a rage by comma splices; they will give themselves a hernia with fury, and will cover your essay in red pen.

Oddly enough, this quirk was tolerated more in the nineteenth century. So, you will sometimes see comma splices used in writing by very stylish and correct writers, such as Robert Louis Stevenson or Ralph Waldo Emerson. However, their works would now get red pen all over them. This just proves that the language is alive and constantly changing, but it is not worth arguing this point with your tutor. Learn the current rules and follow them.

My experience as a marker suggests that the comma splice is a common mistake of bright students who read quickly and think coherently. Sometimes certain ideas seem so connected that one instinctively wants to put them in the same sentence. However, linking these is no longer the job of the comma. If you really want to run together two sentences that seem to connect, consider a semi-colon. It is an under-used punctuation resource. Alternatively, include a conjunction: **and, but, so, or**. Connective adverbs, such as **however, yet, still, nevertheless, therefore, thus** and **moreover** are not strong enough to join two sentences. If you want to use one of these, stop the sentence and start again. If you are a quick reader, keep a special lookout for comma splices as you proofread.

Quick fix

- Put apostrophes in the right places. It is easy when you know the rules.
- **It's** should never appear in your essay. If you mean **it is**, write this out in full. If you mean **its = belonging to it**, there is no apostrophe.
- Avoid comma splices; use a semi-colon or start a new sentence. Keep an eye open for comma splices when you proofread your essay.
- Use commas instead of brackets if you want to include extra information in parenthesis in a sentence.

13 polish up your punctuation

In this chapter you will learn:
- how to use semi-colons and colons
- where to put dashes and hyphens
- how to use brackets, quotation marks and exclamation marks.

More punctuation

Some people understand how to use commas and full stops, but fall apart when they try to handle other types of punctuation. Many mistakes in essays are caused by students trying to use semi-colons, dashes and colons without properly understanding how these punctuation marks work. This chapter explains the basic rules for some more punctuation marks, and gives some guidance on how these should be used in your work.

Semi-colons

Few people know how to use a semi-colon well, which is a pity, as this is an elegant element of style, which can be used to create beautifully balanced sentences. It has two main functions in prose:

- **to connect two sentences.** This is a good antidote to the comma splice. It works especially well for short sentences where the sense follows on directly into the second sentence, and where the two halves are of equal importance and length:

  ✓ I opened the book; I began to read.

  It is also possible to use a semi-colon with a connective adverb:

  ✓ I opened the book; however, I did not begin to read.

  This is more cumbersome and should be used sparingly. The golden rule of using semi-colons to join clauses is that each half of the completed sentence should also operate as a grammatical sentence in its own right. In other words, only use a semi-colon where you could put a full stop. Therefore, you should avoid putting a semi-colon next to conjunctions, such as **and, but** and **so,** or relatives, such as **that, which** and **when.** You do not need these. The semi-colon does the job of linking well enough by itself.

- **to separate items on a list.** This is especially useful when the list is long and the individual items on the list include commas:

  ✓ Quantitative research has many strengths: it allows researchers to consider a large number of responses, thus giving a broad view of the issue; it encourages the application of rigorous, systematic analysis; it enables researchers to observe shifting trends over a period of time.

This way the reader can easily tell where the important divisions between the items occur. If this list only contained commas, it would be very confusing. When using semi-colons in a list, it is a good idea to introduce the list with a colon to show where the list begins.

Colons

Like semi-colons, these are rarely used but are not as confusing as many people think. The function of a colon is to introduce information of some kind:

- **to introduce a list.** A colon announces that something important is about to follow. This makes it ideal for kicking off a long list, as above. The list can also be a sequence of short items separated by commas:

  ✓ cake requires four ingredients: flour, sugar, butter and eggs.

- **to introduce a quotation or speech.** This is very useful in essays, and works well before a large, indented quotation. Always use a colon to introduce a quotation which follows a complete sentence. There are plenty of examples on these pages.

- **to introduce an explanation or statement.** In this case the colon is used to create some sort of anticipation. It is often used when reporting speech or when summarizing or expanding the first half of the sentence:

  ✓ Austen's message is clear: money is an essential element in a happy marriage.

or

  ✓ Elizabeth makes her feelings obvious: she despises Mr Collins.

Unlike the semi-colon, the colon does not always require two equally balanced clauses. In fact it works most powerfully when it is used to introduce a single word or a short, punchy phrase:

  ✓ However, Austen's heroines desire something more than money: love.

✓ Elizabeth feels only one emotion for Mr Collins: contempt.

This construction also works in reverse:

✓ Contempt: this is the only emotion Elizabeth feels for Mr Collins.

This is very striking and, as with all grammatical flourishes, should be used occasionally and with caution. Try this no more than once a term.

Dashes

Unlike semi-colons and colons, dashes are over-used. They are often used by writers who are unsure which punctuation mark to choose. Dashes should not be used instead of brackets, parenthetical commas, semi-colons, full stops, or colons before lists and quotations. Avoid all of the following constructions:

✗ Elizabeth – an independent young woman – is in no hurry to marry.

✗ Elizabeth makes her feelings obvious – she despises Mr Collins.

✗ Elizabeth feels only one emotion for Mr Collins – contempt.

All of these can be rewritten using more appropriate punctuation. However, dashes do have their place, whatever some may say. When you use one make sure you type a long dash (–) not a short hyphen (-). Press Ctrl, Alt and the hyphen key at the top right of your keyboard. Alternatively, if you are working in a Word programme, you can type two short hyphens, (--) without spaces, between the two words on either side. When you hit the space bar at the end of the second word, the two hyphens will be converted to a long dash. Dashes are useful where the sense of the sentence is interrupted in some way, or where a long qualification or description has led away from the main point of the sentence. The dash provides a breathing space in which the sentence can reorganize itself:

✓ Elizabeth Bennett is young, attractive, intelligent, vivacious, independent to the point of stubbornness – the classic Austen heroine.

The final phrase does not fit easily into the syntax of the sentence, but it is obviously referring to the subject of the sentence, Elizabeth Bennett. If you were to put a comma after 'stubbornness', the final phrase would get lost in the list of adjectives. You could create a new sentence: 'She is the classic Austen heroine.' However, this lacks the immediacy and movement of the first version. A dash seems justified in this case. Here is another one:

✓ Hamlet's indecisiveness, his arrogance, his suspicion of others, his passionate, brooding, introspective nature – these all contribute to his downfall.

In both these sentences you could quite correctly substitute a colon. However, the effect of a colon is to lead the reader forward into the following section. A dash is more like a bucket of cold water flung in the reader's face, jolting them back to the starting point of the sentence. Nobody wants this experience too often, so, once more, use with extreme caution. If you can replace a dash with another punctuation mark, you probably should.

Hyphens

Hyphens have a completely different role from dashes, so try not to get them mixed up. A hyphen is a short mark (-) used to connect two words into a single compound word: **mid-September, set-up, post-Darwinian, second-hand, acid-free.** You can test out whether or not you need the hyphen by thinking about whether each of the words could be applied separately to the thing you are describing or if the sense of the sentence would be changed by splitting these words up. Acid-free paper is not the same thing as acid paper. Nor is it the same as free paper. The two words need to be linked or the meaning disappears. You need a hyphen here.

Some compound words do not need the hyphen and are written as 'solid' words: **postgraduate, underhand, midwinter, milkman, transatlantic.** If you are in doubt about the word you want to use, look it up in the dictionary. Sometimes a hyphen is needed when you are adding a prefix to a word, especially if this results in a double vowel: **re-evaluation, co-operation, pre-empt.** You also need a hyphen if the newly formed word could be confused with another word: **re-creation** is not the same as **recreation.** Also consider **re-count** and **recount; re-sign** and **resign; re-act** and **react; re-source** and **resource.**

Some phrases seem to require hyphens in some cases but not in others, for example: **long-term, fourteenth-century, five-year-old**. This can be confusing, but there is a logical explanation. These phrases are usually adjective-noun combinations. These require a hyphen when they are being used as adjective phrases immediately before another noun. The hyphen makes clear to which noun the adjective is connected. You would not need hyphens to say:

> This will be a benefit in the long term.

> The Renaissance flourished in Florence in the fourteenth century.

> Her son is five years old.

However, if you turn these sentences around to put the adjective-noun combination immediately before the other noun as an adjective phrase, you should use hyphens.

> This will be a long-term benefit.

> The Renaissance flourished in fourteenth-century Florence.

> She has a five-year-old son.

You should also use hyphens for fractions and numbers under one hundred if you are writing these out in full: **three-quarters, twenty-eight, ninety-nine, one hundred and twenty-one, four thousand and forty-two**.

You do not need hyphens if the adjective phrase is the name of a person or place with capital letters, for example: **North Sea** oil, a **Mary Quant** dress, an **Italo Calvino** novel, a **Peter Pan** complex, a **John Singer Sargent** painting.

Top tip

Working at a screen is hard on your eyes and your back. Take a short break at least once every hour. Stand up, walk about a bit and put the kettle on. You will make fewer mistakes and feel less stressed.

Quotation marks

In British usage, speech and quotations are signalled by single quote marks:

✓ Dickens begins *A Christmas Carol* with a ghostly reference: 'Marley was dead: to begin with. There is no doubt whatever about that.'

Quotations and speech within quotations are signalled by double quote marks:

✓ '"Bah!" said Scrooge, "Humbug!"'

You will see this done the other way around, with double quote marks on the outside and single quotes within. This will probably be in books or journals published in the US, where the system is reversed. Please use the system of the country where you are writing.

If you have quoted a complete sentence, put any punctuation inside the quotation marks. This shows that the quote is complete in itself. For example:

✓ She said, 'This essay is very well written.'

If you have quoted a part of a sentence, put the punctuation outside the quotation marks. This shows that the quote needs the rest of the sentence to make sense:

✓ She said that the essay was 'very well written'.

In US usage punctuation always goes inside quotation marks. As before, use the system appropriate and be consistent. For more on quotations and quotation marks, see Chapter 17.

Brackets

You will need to use a lot of brackets in your work to give clear and accurate references. So, try to avoid using them for anything else (such as asides to your reader, like this one). As I noted in the previous chapter, you can use commas to add an extra phrase in the middle of a sentence. See page 116. You should also avoid using dashes for this purpose. If you use brackets within your text as well as for reference material, your text can become very cluttered and hard to follow. On the whole, you should try to avoid putting any information into parentheses, even if you do think it is fascinating or entertaining.

Question marks

Make sure you have a question mark at the end of every question. However, try not to fill your essay with too many questions. Asking a question can be a rather lazy way of introducing new material. A run of several questions in the one paragraph is rather exhausting for your reader. It can also make you sound as though you do not yet know the answers. Try to avoid constructions like this:

✗ First we need to ask, what did Darwin say? What shaped his thinking? Why was his work so important?

Indirect questions can provide a better way to raise issues which you wish to address in your essay. These do not need a question mark:

✓ First it is essential to ask What Darwin said, what shaped his thinking, and why his work was so important.

Remember that your essay is an answer to a question, not a series of more questions. So use questions sparingly. If you have to ask them, make sure that you answer them.

Exclamation marks

Do not use these unless they appear in quotations. An academic essay does not exclaim or insist. It reasons and persuades.

Ask yourself

- When should I use a semi-colon?
- What is the difference between a dash and a hyphen?
- Have I asked too many questions?
- What is in my brackets?

Quick fix

- Semi-colons are for linking two complete statements. Only use a semi-colon where you could use a full stop.
- Use colons to introduce a statement, a quotation or a list.
- Avoid peppering your text with too many dashes. Use another punctuation mark if you can.
- Use hyphens for numbers between twenty-one and ninety-nine, for adjective phrases and for some compound words. Look these up in the dictionary if you are unsure whether you need a hyphen.
- Be careful with quotation marks. Think about whether your punctuation should be inside or outside quotation marks.

14

make sentences make sense

In this chapter you will learn:
- how to write sentences that make sense
- how to handle clauses and agreement.

Getting to grips with grammar

Language needs grammar. It is essential if you want to construct any kind of statement beyond simply naming objects. If you want to express interesting ideas then a sound grasp of grammar is required. Your understanding of grammar may be more developed than you realize. If you have studied a foreign language, you may have a very sophisticated knowledge of how it operates. Many students use grammar well without knowing all the terms for the techniques they are using. This is fine when it works, but if you do not know the vocabulary of grammar it can be hard to stand back and analyse where a sentence went wrong. Markers tend to use technical, grammatical terms when pointing out problems in your work, which is not much use to you if you do not know what they are talking about. This chapter will highlight a few common problems, and offer definitions of some terms that may crop up in your markers' comments. If you have serious problems with grammar, this book will not solve them. If your markers consistently complain about your syntax, sentence structure, tenses, pronouns and the like, you probably need some help from a study-skills tutor or to get hold of a book specifically about grammar. See pages 204–5 for some suggestions of further reading.

Clauses

Clauses are the internal sections of a sentence, which fit together to build up meaning. Every clause has a noun and a verb or, if you prefer, a thing and an action. These are sometimes called the subject and the predicate. However, not all clauses are of equal weight and value. The clauses of a sentence are like the internal walls of a house. Some can be moved around or altered without doing too much damage. One is always essential and cannot be removed without the whole thing falling in. Clauses which are essential are **main clauses**. A compound sentence (see page 115) will have two main clauses. A main clause requires a noun and a verb:

I know.

However, it can also be more elaborate:

I know some useful things about grammar.

A main clause is the part of a sentence which can make a sentence all by itself. 'Know' is the **principal verb** of this sentence, which means it is the verb in the main clause. 'I' is the **subject** of the sentence. This means it is the noun doing the verb, also called the **predicate**. 'Some useful things about grammar' forms the **object** of the sentence. This is the noun phrase which represents the thing that 'I know'. Subjects, objects and predicates can all be made up of single words or phrases to make up a main clause.

Subordinate clauses

On to this main clause one can attach other clauses which support and describe the main clause. These are called **subordinate clauses**. All the subordinate clauses in the following examples are in bold. Subordinate clauses can often be moved around without changing the meaning of a sentence:

I know some useful things about grammar, **which is lucky for you.**

or

It is lucky for you that I know some useful things about grammar.

A subordinate clause is a section of a sentence which contains a subject and a predicate (i.e. a noun and a verb), but which is doing the job of an adverb or an adjective. It is not part of the main action of the sentence. It is describing a thing or an action in the main clause or in another subordinate clause. A sentence can have more than one subordinate clause. They can follow and/or precede the main clause.

Because I have studied English, I know some useful things about grammar, **which is lucky for you, as you can draw on these to improve your writing.**

By now, however, this sentence is getting a bit long and complex for my liking. Once you have more than three clauses in a sentence, it is very easy to get muddled up about which is the important one. I advise against sentences any more complex than this. They are hard to write well and hard work to read. The real danger is that the main clause is missed out, and you end up with something like this:

✗ Because I have studied English, which is lucky for you, as you can draw on these to improve your writing.

This is not a sentence. It has no main verb, only a succession of subordinate clauses. A subordinate clause is often flagged up by a word such as **while, which, if, that, whenever, although, as, despite**. This kind of clause describes the subject, the object or the predicate of the main clause. A phrase containing a **participle** (usually a verb ending in **–ing**) behaves similarly. These cannot form sentences in their own right, even though you may see it done in the Sunday papers and in novels. In your written work, therefore, you should avoid things like this:

✗ Although this is not the case.
✗ However much you try.
✗ Rarely appearing to do so.
✗ Being of sound mind and judgement.

All of these are **sentence fragments**. They do have nouns and verbs, but they lack a principal verb and are not valid as stand-alone sentences in formal written English. They have no place in academic essays. The Microsoft grammar check will not always pick up sentence fragments, so you need to correct these carefully yourself.

Dangling elements

You also need to make sure that the different parts of the sentence match up in a way that makes sense. A subordinate clause or participle phrase can cause complications when it is not quite clear to which bit of the main clause it refers. For example:

> **While she was writing** *The Voyage Out,* Virginia Woolf's sister Vanessa Bell painted her portrait.

This is called a **dangling clause,** because the 'while' clause dangles ambiguously from the main clause, which it should modify and clarify. This sentence suggests that Virginia Woolf's sister wrote *The Voyage Out,* which is not the case. It also fails to make clear whose portrait was painted. In this sort of sentence, try to keep the subject of the main clause as the subject of the subordinate clause, so that the two halves of the sentence are talking about the same thing or person. This may require some rewording.

> While Virginia Woolf was writing *The Voyage Out,* she sat for a portrait painted by her sister Vanessa Bell.

This is clearer. However, it is also possible to solve this kind of problem by writing shorter sentences:

> Vanessa Bell painted a portrait of her sister, Virginia Woolf. During this period, Woolf was writing *The Voyage Out*.

Look out for other elements in sentences that 'dangle'. Make it clear what each part of the sentence describes. Remember that pronouns usually refer to the most recent available noun. (See the section on pronouns on page 139.) Make sure that what you have written makes sense to your reader, not just to you.

Relative clauses

A relative clause is a subordinate clause which refers to a preceding noun or pronoun. It usually starts with **who, which** or **that**:

> The play **which we studied last year** is out of print.

Relative clauses can be divided into two kinds: **defining** and **non-defining**.

A **defining relative clause** is essential to the meaning of the sentence because it gives important information about the preceding word. This identifies it in some way, marking it out from all other possible occurrences of the word. The example above is a defining relative clause. It makes clear that the sentence is discussing one particular play studied last year, in contrast to any other plays studied this year or two years ago.

A **non-defining relative clause** offers information that describes but does not specify; it is doing the same job as a modifying clause in parenthesis (see pages 116–17). Like this, it must be enclosed in commas to keep it out of the way of the main action of the sentence:

✓ Shakespeare, **who was born in 1564,** wrote poetry as well as plays.

When the clause defines, there are no commas. When it does not, it is surrounded by commas, or by a comma and a full stop, if it ends the sentence. Remember to add the second comma after a non-defining relative clause. Avoid things like this:

✗ Shakespeare, who was born in 1564 wrote poetry as well as plays.

It is important to decide whether a relative clause is defining or non-defining, since the commas alone can change the meaning completely. Compare the two pairs of sentences below:

He answered all the questions which were on Shakespeare.

or

He answered all the questions, which were on Shakespeare.

Were all the available questions on Shakespeare or not? My personal favourite in this category is:

All the sailors who were in the lifeboat were saved.

or

All the sailors, who were in the lifeboat, were saved.

The first sentence implies that some sailors did not make it into the lifeboat and came to a sorry end. The other one says that all the sailors were in the lifeboat and survived. Who says that punctuation is not a matter of life and death?

Top tip

Keep your sentences short. You will make fewer mistakes with grammar. Look carefully at any sentence that takes up more than three lines of text. If it would read better as two sentences, then change it.

That and which

If you use your Microsoft grammar check as you write, you will find that it constantly makes a fuss about whether you use 'that' or 'which' at the beginning of relative clauses. The people at Microsoft, for reasons of their own, will not let you start a defining relative clause with 'which'. If you type a 'which' without a comma before it, a green line appears under the text. Microsoft insists on:

The play **that** we studied last year is out of print.

or

He answered all the questions **that** were on Shakespeare.

You can do it this way for a quiet life, but the rule above about commas is the important one. I reserve the right to use 'that' and 'which' in both defining and non-defining clauses as appropriate. You should too.

Agreement

Agreement is all about making sure that the different parts of a sentence match up, so that the whole thing makes sense. The most common mistake in this area is a failure to make the subject noun and the main verb agree. A singular subject should have a singular verb. A plural subject should have a plural verb. This sounds simple, but can be confusing when the subject of the sentence is a short phrase rather than one word:

✗ The number of passes **have** risen to fifty.

This sentence is really about 'the number'. So, the verb should be **has**:

✓ The number of passes **has** risen to fifty.

'The number' is the main subject of the sentence. The phrase 'of passes' is only a modifier of the subject. 'Number' is singular and requires a singular verb. However, a phrase containing 'a number of' would take a plural verb, just like a phrase containing **a lot of** before a plural noun:

✓ A number of passes **are** just above the borderline.

✓ A lot of passes **are** just above the borderline.

This is because **a number of** and **a lot of** behave like modifiers, such as 'many'. Be especially careful of this issue if you have a list in a sentence, or some sort of qualifying or relative clause:

✗ Hamlet's failure to take control of the situation, act decisively, and regain his rightful position as ruler, **are** disastrous.

Hamlet's 'failure' is the subject of the sentence. So this should read:

✓ Hamlet's failure to take control of the situation, act decisively, and regain his rightful position as ruler, **is** disastrous.

Collective nouns

Some writers relax the rule about singular subject, singular verb for collective nouns. These nouns denote groups and therefore imply their members, such as **army, audience, committee, family** and **jury.** It is often acceptable to say:

My family **are** delightful.

But if you start this sort of thing, it can be hard to know where to stop. What about the **government,** the **university,** the **school,** the **academic community,** the **fire brigade,** or the **company?** For the sake of consistency and accuracy, it is better to stick to the singular rule and to write:

✓ My family **is** delightful.

If you want to make it clear that you are talking about the multiple members of the group then do so. Use a phrase such as:

✓ All the members of my family **are** delightful.

See the following chapter for some advice about how to handle this sort of sentence when it includes an indefinite pronoun such as **everybody, someone, anybody, nobody, none.**

Tenses

Tenses also need to correspond if your sentences are going to make sense. Although you can include more than one tense in a sentence, make sure that you have it clear in your own head when things happen. You should also ensure that it is clear to your reader whether things happened in the past or are continuing into the present. Be especially careful with conditional cases and reported speech. As with everything else, look carefully at what you are writing. Make sure that you know what you want to say and that it cannot be read in a different way.

Ask yourself

- Do all my sentences make sense?
- Do I have any long sentences which I should consider splitting?
- Does everything agree in my sentences?

Quick fix

- Think about clauses. Do not have too many in one sentence. It is always better to write short, clear sentences whenever possible. Do not present subordinate clauses as complete sentences. These are sentence fragments.

- Look out for dangling clauses at the beginning of a sentence which do not match up with what follows. Start your sentence with the main clause wherever possible.

- Do not rely on Microsoft to sort out your grammar. Learn to think for yourself about whether what you have written makes sense.

- Make sure that single nouns have single verbs and plural nouns have plural verbs.

15

grammar that works

In this chapter you will learn:
- how to handle pronouns
- some more hints and tips for using grammar.

Pronouns

Pronouns are the words in a sentence which do the job of filling in for a noun or a noun phrase which could be there instead. For example, take a sentence with three nouns:

The boy handed **the book** to **the girl**.

Any of these nouns can be substituted for a pronoun.

He handed the book to the girl.

He handed **it** to the girl.

He handed **it** to **her**.

Remember that pronouns can also fill in for proper names, abstract ideas, or groups of people and things. Any noun can be replaced with a pronoun. When you are constructing a sentence with one or more pronouns, try to bear in mind what each of the pronouns is representing and make this clear to your reader. This can help you to avoid some basic errors.

Which noun is it?

A pronoun always refers to the most recent plausible noun. This is called the **law of antecedents**. It works like this:

The cat dropped the mouse. It ran away.

This says that the mouse ran away, not the cat. However a gendered pronoun will match up with the most recent gendered noun, or proper name.

The girl dropped the mouse. She ran away.

In this case it is the girl who runs away. Technically, of course, it might be a female mouse. However, we are not told the mouse's gender, so the girl is the most likely candidate for **she**.

Pronouns can get out of hand when there are too many of them in a sentence, especially if the sentence contains an indefinite pronoun or two, such as **it** and **this**. For example, what does this mean?

It is useful to note that Hamlet's indecision about killing his uncle takes more time than it should, but this does not mean that it is morally wrong, and this might be the case because he is able to think about it first.

Is it Hamlet's indecision or the killing of his uncle that may or may not be wrong? What might be the case? Who is able to think about it first: Hamlet or his uncle? A student who writes a sentence like this may have an idea in their own head what they mean, but they have not exactly made their point clear. On the whole, you should avoid starting sentences with **it** and **this** whenever possible, and be aware that pronouns used later in a sentence may be misread if not clearly attached to an earlier noun. There is no law against using a noun or name twice in a sentence if it helps clarify the point. Always strike out pointless phrases such as 'it is useful to note that'. Write shorter, clearer sentences.

I and me

In speech and in writing, people are often confused about the difference between **I** and **me**, especially if these are paired up with another noun. For example:

✗ **Me** and my sister went to town.

✗ The taxi came to collect my sister and **I**.

This happens because there has been a mix-up about which pronoun is the subject of the sentence. You should use **I** as the subject of the sentence. When **I** is the person doing the action, then **I** is the subject of the sentence. You should use **me** as the object of the sentence. When something happens to **me**, then **me** is the object of the sentence. This remains the same whether there is an extra person added in or not. You would not say:

✗ **Me** went to town.

or

✗ The taxi came to collect **I**.

So the correct usage is:

✓ My sister and **I** went to town.

and

✓ The taxi came to collect my sister and **me**.

Who and whom

Many writers have a similar problem with **who** and **whom**. **Who** should be used when the noun that **who** represents is the subject of the sentence or clause in which it appears. **Whom** should be used when the noun it represents is the object of the sentence or clause. For example:

✗ I have a brother **whom** lives in London.
✗ **Who** does this belong to?

For some reason most people have a lot less trouble with this issue in relation to **he** and **she**, or **him** and **her**. So you can use these pronouns to work out whether you need **who** or **whom**. Rethink the sentence with a personal pronoun and you will be able to decide whether it is a subject or an object:

✓ **He** lives in London.
✓ This belongs to **him**.

He, she and **I** are all subject pronouns, so replace these with **who**.

✓ I have a brother **who** lives in London.

Him, her and **me** are all object pronouns, so replace these with **whom**.

✓ **Whom** does this belong to?

This example includes a preposition: **to**. Prepositions are words which tell you the relationship of one noun or pronoun to another. It can help to think of these as placing words, which tell you where things are, for example: **in, with, by, from, up, at, on**. Prepositions are often clues that you should be using **whom** rather than **who**. For example: **to whom, by whom, with whom, from whom**. It will be easier to work out whether you need **who** or **whom** if you organize the sentence so that the preposition and the pronoun stay together:

✓ To **whom** does this belong?

There is more about rephrasing sentences ending in prepositions later in this chapter.

Indefinite pronouns

In the previous chapter I explained that collective nouns should have a singular verb. The same applies to indefinite pronouns such as **everybody, everyone, somebody, someone, anybody, anyone, nobody, no one** and **none**. For example:

✓ Everybody in my family **is** delightful.

Watch out when the indefinite pronoun is used after a plural.

✗ None of my relatives **are** delightful.
✓ None of my relatives **is** delightful.

This seems counter-intuitive until you remember that 'none' is just a short version of 'not one.' All the indefinite pronouns listed above follow this rule. However, they are sometimes linked to the plurals **they, their** and **them(selves)**:

> Everybody is entitled to **their** opinion.

or

> If someone does not like poetry, I would not make **them** read it.

This is done to avoid a gendered pronoun which makes an assumption about whether the 'someone' is male or female. In earlier centuries **his** or **him** was often used in this context as an indefinite pronoun. However, as many people pointed out, this excluded half the population from this sort of sentence. One can say 'his or her' and 'him or her', but it sounds a bit clumsy, and raises the problem of who should go first: girls or boys? Many other languages have a non-gendered pronoun, a human version of **it,** for this sort of situation, but English does not. Some older writers object to **their, theirs** and **them** in this context, but the language is definitely moving towards this as the solution to the problem. On the whole, I think this is better than trying to turn the clock back to a sexist way of seeing the world.

Top tip

Back up your essay document file every time you stop for a break. Then, even if your computer system crashes while you are working, you will never lose more than a couple of hours' work.

Sentences ending in a preposition

This is one of those issues that gets some markers in a rage. Earlier I explained that prepositions show the relationship of one noun to another. For example: **in, with, by, from, up, at, on**. In formal English you should avoid ending a sentence or clause with a preposition:

✗ This is an issue which city councils should look **at**.
✗ There is nothing to be afraid **of**.
✗ That is an error which she will not put **up with**.

This sort of construction often works well enough in speech, but in writing it is not good practice because the preposition ends up a long way from the word which it is meant to be placing. This can be confusing, especially in a long, complex sentence. The textbook way to resolve this issue is to put the preposition earlier in the sentence.

✓ This is an issue **at** which city councils should look.
✓ There is nothing **of** which to be afraid.

However, this can sound very cumbersome, especially in a sentence such as the one below where two prepositions are run together:

That is an error **up with** which she will not put.

Technically this is correct, but it sounds ludicrous. So, this is not recommended. If moving the preposition would leave you with a really awkward sentence, then you will have to balance up whether you want to rewrite it or not. You can often get around this problem by reorganizing the sentence or choosing a different verb which does not require a preposition. Usually this will lead to a neater and stronger sentence, so it is probably worth doing.

✓ City councils should look at this issue.
✓ There is nothing to fear.
✓ That is an error which she will not tolerate.

Always look for ways in which you can make your language smoother and stronger.

Split infinitives

An infinitive is the root form of the verb. In English this is signalled by **to,** followed by the verb. For example: **to** walk, **to** run, **to** see, **to** go.

I wanted **to go** to the cinema **to see** a film.

In this sentence **to** is used three times. The first use, **to go,** is an infinitive. The third use, **to see,** is another infinitive. However, the second use, **to the cinema,** is a preposition, which places I in relation to **the cinema.** When **to** is followed by a noun or pronoun, it will usually be working as a preposition. When **to** is followed by a verb, it will usually be working as an infinitive. In an infinitive, **to** is an integral part of the verb phrase. A split infinitive is when something comes between **to** and the verb. The most celebrated example of a split infinitive comes from *Star Trek*, where the crew of the Starship Enterprise aim

to **boldy** go where no man has gone before.

Usually the word that gets in the way is an adverb which describes the verb. For example: **quickly, completely, badly, well, also, never.** The way to fix this is to move the adverb before the **to** or after the verb. Either is correct:

✓ boldly to go where no man has gone before
✓ never to say goodbye
✓ to fare badly
✓ to write well

Ask yourself

• Which pronoun do I need?
• What is the subject of my sentence?
• Have I tried always to avoid split infinitives?

Keep it clear

The point of grammar is to keep language tidy and working smoothly so that it is easier to understand. Look critically at every sentence you write. Make sure that your words cannot be read another way from the way that you intend. If they could be misunderstood, rewrite the sentence so that it makes sense.

Quick fix

- Use pronouns with care. Make sure that the pronoun refers to the most recent available noun. Check that you have chosen the right pronoun to match up with the person or thing you are talking about.
- Avoid vague pronouns such as 'this' and 'it', especially at the start of sentences. Too many of these will make your essay very vague and confusing to read.
- Avoid placing prepositions at the end of a sentence, but do not tie your sentence in knots in order to do so. If necessary, rephrase the sentence.
- Avoid split infinitives. Move the adverb before or after the verb phrase.

16

spelling

Look it up

There is no short cut to good spelling. You just have to learn what each word in the language looks like. However, there is one simple thing you can do which will help: buy a dictionary. A good dictionary will be the most useful book you buy during your time as a student, so do not begrudge the money for it. However, there is no point spending a week's rent on a leather-bound, two-volume, deluxe dictionary. Buy a small, compact dictionary, ideally less than 20 cm tall, that is light enough and sturdy enough to travel in your rucksack. A dictionary on the bookshelf at home is no use if you are working in the library or the computing centre. Get into the habit of taking your dictionary with you when you are writing, and look up words you are unsure about. This will not just help with your spelling; make sure that you also read and understand the definition of the words you use. It is easy to confuse similar words. Using a dictionary rather than the spell check on your PC can help you avoid some embarrassing errors.

Checking your spelling

Microsoft spell check is a useful function, and can help you spot typing errors that your eye might otherwise miss. However, it is not foolproof. It will not notice the difference between **their** and **there,** or **it** and **is,** or **allusive** and **elusive.** It will clear anything that it finds in its own dictionary, without checking to see if this word belongs in your sentence. If you rely on it too heavily, you can end up with sentences like this:

> During this scene, the ghost of Hamlet's father can be seen hoovering in the background.

or

> In *Paradise Lost,* Satan rallies the fallen angles.

Do not automatically accept any corrections that the spell check suggests. Be especially careful with names. A final-year student at my university recently submitted an essay where the names of two biblical figures, Hagar and Ishmael, had been changed throughout to 'Haggard' and 'Fishmeal'. How we laughed.

The spell check function cannot help you with technical terms or proper names, so look at these very carefully, especially if you are dealing with scientific terms, names of chemicals, anatomical terms or medicines. A misplaced letter or two might dramatically change the meaning of your whole project.

Always read through your essay carefully after you have printed it out. You will notice mistakes that you did not pick up on screen. If there are only a few of these, your marker will not mind if you correct these by hand. It is better to show that you have read through your work than to present a pristine text full of errors. If you find a lot of mistakes, go back, make corrections and print out the essay again. Remember that the ability to produce a clean, polished text is an important skill in its own right. It is worth spending time and effort on this. Good spellers are hard to find these days and are a valuable asset in any profession.

Common errors

There may be no short cut to good spelling, but there are some obvious pitfalls which you can avoid. Here are some areas which need special care:

words ending:	-ant/ent	e.g. dependant, dependent
	-ary/ery	e.g. stationary, stationery
	-ance/ence	e.g. observance, correspondence
	-ite/ate	e.g. infinite, obstinate
	-ible/able	e.g. fallible, reasonable
	-ibility/ability	eg: fallibility, disability
	-arate/erate	e.g. separate, desperate
	-ege/edge	e.g. privilege, acknowledge
	-cede/ceed/sede	e.g. precede, proceed, supersede
	-ice/ise	e.g. noun 'practice', verb 'practise'
words beginning:	de/di-	e.g. despair, divide
	im/in-	e.g. impossible, inconceivable
words including:	-ie/ei	e.g. achieve, believe, receive

In this case, the old rule is a good one: 'I before E except after C, when the sound is E.')

-our   e.g. vigour/vigorous

(This often becomes **or** before a suffix at the end of a word; **our** sometimes becomes **or** in US spellings – see below.)

-double letters	e.g travel/travelled/ travelling, trap/trapped/ trapping
	Single letters at the end of a verb are sometimes doubled when a suffix is added at the end of the word. This does not happen in US spelling (see below).
words that sound like other words:	e.g. principle/principal, affect/effect, allude/elude

Remember to trust your dictionary, not your ears.

Top tips

Buy a handbook of key technical terms for your subject and keep this near you as you work. If you cannot find a book like this, check the spellings of your technical language against academic books or journal articles.

Capitals

Proper nouns (names) such as England, France, Scandinavia, the Thames, Lake Michigan, Mont Blanc, have an initial capital letter. In English, adjectives and nouns denoting nationality and language do as well: English, Old English, Middle English, French, Latin, Italian. Historical periods are treated in the same way: the Middle Ages, the Renaissance.

A common noun is often capitalized when it forms part of a name or a title. Thus the 'History Department' has capitals, but the phrase 'in this department' does not. Claudius in *Hamlet* is 'the King', just as one would write 'the Queen' when referring to Elizabeth II or some other specific queen. But king or queen used in a general way does not have a capital letter. For example, 'The king of a country should not hold too much power'.

God has a capital when one is naming the God of Christian, Islamic or Jewish faiths. Words used as names for God are often capitalized too, such as the Almighty, the Creator, although the practice of capitalizing pronouns referring to God (Him, His,

Thou) is dying out. The 'Gods' of Ancient Greece and Rome also have a capital, although 'gods' from other cultures do not.

Words denoting religions, movements or schools of thought, and peoples, together with the adjectives referring to these, and words denoting people belonging to them, have an initial capital: Christianity, Christian; Dadaism, Dadaist, Dadaistic; Fabianism, Fabianist, Fabian; Islam, Islamic; Jew, Jewish. The Bible, the Old Testament, the New Testament and the Koran all take capitals, as do most book titles. However, the adjective 'biblical' does not.

When typing titles of books, journals, articles, poems and newspapers check the capitalization and copy the style exactly. If **The** is part of the title, then give it a capital T (*The Times*), but if **The** does not appear on the cover of the publication, then keep it lower case (the *Daily Express*). Some books and journal titles are all lower case (*transatlantic review*). Book titles in foreign languages often only capitalize the first letter of the first word (*L'écriture et la différence*). The basic rule is to check the original format and reproduce this. For more advice on how to cite publications, see chapters 19 and 20.

UK and US spellings

Spelling in English differs from country to country. UK spelling is often different from US spelling. Other English-speaking nations tend to follow either the UK or US model, but sometimes have their own variations too. Follow the rules for the country in which you are writing – even if you an international student who learned to spell elsewhere. Remember that you are writing for your reader, not for yourself. Here are a few of the most common differences.

British **ll**/American **l**: A single consonant at the end of a word is often doubled before a suffix in UK English, but not in US English: travelling/traveling, revelling/reveling.

British **re**/American **er**: centre/center, metre/meter, theatre/theater.

British **ogue**/American **og**: catalogue/catalog, demagogue/demagog.

British **our**/American **or**: colour/color, humour/humor, vigour/vigor.

If you are quoting from a text which was originally written and printed in another country, it is acceptable to reproduce the text as it appears on the page. For example, if you are in the UK, but wish to quote Robert Frost's poem 'The Road Not Taken', use the US spelling.

> Two roads diverged in a wood, and I –
> I took the one less traveled by,
> And that has made all the difference.

(Frost, 2001, p.105)

Quick fix

- Buy a dictionary and use it. Keep it beside you as you write and look up anything about which you are unsure – several times if necessary.
- Do not rely on the spellcheck function to sort out your spelling. It will not spot all your mistakes, and the suggestions it will make may not help you much.
- Correct your work carefully. Learn which words are most likely to be misspelled and pay special attention to these.

Try it out: using language

Put the apostrophes in the correct places in the following sentences:

1 Its time that the cat had its dinner.
2 Theyre getting the ship ready for its first voyage.
3 Hes so tall hell bang his head if he doesnt watch out.
4 Its a pity that Jamess sister cant come to the childrens party.
5 Weve asked Carolines brother to find out whos coming.

Use commas, semi-colons and colons to mark the clauses in these sentences so that they make sense:

1 Not only is it damp and cold it is also dark.
2 However difficult it seems at first driving a car like riding a bicycle soon becomes second nature.
3 However you require a lot of practice which can take a long time.
4 The books which were on the shelf had not been read.

5 There are three things you need to do clean out the fireplace lay a new fire with wood coal paper and firelighters and light it with the matches.

Add capitals and punctuation to the following paragraph.

brooklyn bridge which links the island of manhattan to long island was opened in 1883 and quickly became an iconic feature of the new york skyline not only was the bridge an ambitious engineering project which showed that americas technological and industrial capabilities had grown to equal those of its european competitors the bridge was also a symbol of the fast developing nations ideals and aspirations at the bridges opening abram s hewitt a congressman and industrialist celebrated the new structure as a sign of mans ability to subdue nature he said it stands before us today as the sum and epitome of human knowledge brooklyn bridge has featured prominently in american art literature and film from its opening to the twenty first century.

Answers can be found on pages 201–2.

part

four
using sources

17

making sources work

In this chapter you will learn:
- the difference between primary and secondary sources
- how to use sources effectively.

Go to the source

Effective use of source material is crucial. Chapter 06 discussed where to find good resources. However, selecting and reading good source material is only part of using sources well. Part Four of this book will show you how to present your material effectively. This chapter explores a few strategies for using your material to strengthen your argument. It also looks at the kind of language you should use when discussing other scholars' work. Chapter 18 shows you how to avoid plagiarism. Chapters 19 and 20 explain how to reference your work properly. Remember that using sources well is about much more than keeping on the right side of plagiarism regulations or writing tidy references. It is about showing off your knowledge, and making your sources work to back up your ideas.

It is almost impossible to write a really good essay or dissertation without some use of secondary sources. If you are presenting a report of your own research project, you will need to demonstrate that you have looked at relevant scholarship. If you are constructing a formal essay or a literature review, then source material will probably form the central element of your project. Even if you are writing a critical analysis or a learning log, which may not call for direct use of secondary sources, you will produce a better piece of work if you have a good knowledge of a range of background material and recent scholarship in your area of study. Learning from other thinkers and writers is what studying is all about, and reading other people's work can sharpen up your own ideas. However, you need to know how to incorporate other writers' work into your own. Good use of secondary material shows that you have done your research, and that you are confident about your own opinions. Effective use of source material is often the factor that distinguishes a first-class essay from a high second-class one.

Primary and secondary sources

Source material is often divided into two types: primary and secondary. This division is especially common in subjects with a strong emphasis on studying and analysing texts, such as literature, religious studies, history, law and many social sciences. As its name suggests, primary source material is itself the object of study. Primary source material may include:

- **manuscript material.** For example: the Magna Carta, the Dead Sea Scrolls, the manuscript of a poem by Elizabeth Barrett Browning, a letter from Henry James to his brother William, Watson and Crick's lab notes.
- **published printed material.** For example: a book of historical legal texts, the Bible, a collection of E. B. Browning's poems, the collected letters of Henry and William James, Watson and Crick's published papers, government reports, newspapers and periodicals.
- **objects and works of art.** For example: a collection of nineteenth-century medical instruments, a painting by Hans Holbein, a sculpture by Henry Moore, architectural plans by Edwin Lutyens, a Roman vase excavated in Colchester.

Secondary source material is material that in some way comments on or supports the primary source material. Secondary source material may include:

- **published printed material.** For example: a study of Medieval England, a theological study of the doctrine of incarnation, a critical study of E. B. Browning's poetry, a biography of the James brothers, a study of Watson and Crick's work on DNA, a journal article about the restoration of Hans Holbein's painting *The Ambassadors*, a book about nineteenth-century medicine, a biography of Edwin Lutyens.
- **multimedia material.** For example: an internet journal article on the impact of the Magna Carta on English law, a TV documentary about the finding of the Dead Sea scrolls, a book review of a study of E.B. Browning's poetry, a radio broadcast about the relationship of William and Henry James, a newspaper report of new research on DNA, a film about the life of Edwin Lutyens.

However, these categories are not watertight. Whether a source is primary or secondary depends on how you are using it. For example, if you were working on E. B. Browning's poetry and wanted to quote a remark by Henry James in a letter to his brother, then James's letter would be working as a secondary source. Alternatively, if you were studying documentary making, you might choose to do an analysis of the techniques used in a documentary about the finding of the Dead Sea Scrolls. In this case, the documentary would be the primary object of your study and would be your primary source.

Some tutors like you to list your sources in your bibliography under the separate headings of primary and secondary. Others prefer one list. Whatever your tutor requires, it can be very helpful to think about which source material is central to your project and which material is supportive. Identifying one primary text, or a few primary texts, can help to keep you focused on the point of your project. (See Chapters 19 and 20 for more about bibliographies.)

If your project involves practical research or data gathering and analysis, you are more likely to be using textual material as secondary sources. However, just because this material is called 'secondary' does not mean it is not important. You will need source material to demonstrate your knowledge of different approaches to your topic and to justify your choice of methods.

Create a debate

Use your secondary material to set up a debate within your essay or dissertation. Scholarly literature provides an opportunity for scholars to test out their own ideas and to challenge other people's. Academic journals and publishers host some fiercely fought debates about all kinds of subjects. Try to give a flavour of the cut and thrust of debate in your own discipline in your work.

Chapter 03 explored some strategies for presenting a debate in your subject area in the setting of a literature review. Much of that advice will be relevant here too, so you may want to go back and reread that section. Think of your essay as a round-table discussion on your topic. Try to construct an exciting and controversial interaction. The difference between a literature review and a formal essay in this regard is that, in a literature review, you are chairing this debate and should remain a little detached from the argument. However, in a formal essay your opinion is also on the line, so you should be prepared to take sides if necessary.

Sometimes the kind of debate you want to present will be defined for you by the terms of your essay. For example, look again at the question from Chapter 07: **Critically appraise the potential of both quantitative and qualitative research methods in a rural social science topic.** In this case you need to provide evidence from scholarship which both supports and questions quantitative research methods alongside scholarship which supports and questions qualitative research methods. Some scholarship that helps to bridge or negotiate the gap between them will also be useful in reaching and supporting your conclusion. See the sample plan for this essay on page 67 to see how the source material fitted into the structure of the argument.

However, some questions do not define the debate so neatly. In such cases you will need to pay special attention to your sources as you read and research, in order to get a picture of the differing views and contentious issues connected to your topic.

For example, let's revisit another question from earlier in the book: **What is the relevance of the artist's intention to interpreting works of art?** To somebody who has done very little reading on this subject, it may seem obvious that the artist decides what their painting or sculpture means. However, as soon as you step into the library and find a few books and articles on this issue, you will quickly realize that the debate about artistic and authorial intention is a lively one. In fact, this has been one of the foremost debates in arts and humanities subjects since the 1960s. Your essay should reflect the breadth and passion of this debate, discuss some of the key players and provide sources representing a range of views.

If you are not sure who the key players are in a debate, keep an eye open as you read for names which keep cropping up and for books or papers which are regularly cited. Remember to look in bibliographies and reference lists as well as in texts for ideas of things to read. For example, if most of the articles you are reading about artistic intention mention Roland Barthes' essay 'The Death of the Author', then this is a strong clue that you should track it down and read it.

Try to offer a similar weight and quantity of evidence on each side of the debate to build a balanced essay. However, remember that your job is always to evaluate, to analyse and to come to a conclusion. Do not be afraid to point out weak or outdated material. You want to create a debate in your essay, but you also want to remain in control of your material and your topic. You are pulling the strings, so select and present your material carefully, to show the breadth of your knowledge and to move towards your conclusion.

Take on the experts

Just because someone has spent a lifetime researching a subject and is an internationally recognized authority on a particular subject does not always mean they are right. Feel free to challenge anything and everything that you read. In fact, when you read secondary sources, you should probably start with the assumption that you are going to disagree but you are prepared to be persuaded if the writer makes a good enough case. Apply the principles of critical thinking to your use of sources. Ask probing, testing questions as you read your sources. When you are constructing your argument, think hard about whether your source material strengthens or undermines your own position.

Remember that you do not have to agree with all the material that you use. You are much more likely to create a strong argument if you include some material which presents a perspective opposed to your own, especially if you can show that perspective to be in some way flawed. Students often discard any secondary material with which they disagree and then wonder why their marker complains about an essay that is 'flat' or 'short on analysis'. This is like taking the springs out of a trampoline and then wondering why it does not bounce. If you come across any material that you can prove is missing the point, roll up your sleeves and get to work on it. Just make sure you can back up your position with material from your primary texts, your own research findings or from other scholars. Sometimes pure logic will do the trick too. This is the sort of thing that really makes an essay shine. So, be assertive with experts. They are only human after all.

Acknowledge scholars in your text

Students often drop in a reference or footnote at the end of a sentence, or name a book in the bibliography, and then feel they have adequately dealt with their sources. For example:

> Many critics of the mid-twentieth century see *The Ambassadors* as Henry James's most accomplished novel (Mathiessen, 1944, Beach 1954).

It is especially tempting to slip into this if you are using the author–date/Harvard reference system, which keeps the name of the scholar close to the sentence in which their ideas are being discussed. However, this information is not really integrated into the sense of the sentence, and it can go astray. In the example above, it looks as though the source of information is clear, but in reality it is not always clear which scholar holds which view. For example:

> Critics of the mid-twentieth century disagree whether *The Ambassadors* is Henry James's most accomplished novel or a bad piece of fiction (Matthiessen, 1944, Beach, 1954, Leavis, 1948).

Who said what? You can sometimes solve this sort of problem with some careful placing of references, but references mid-sentence break up the flow of your argument. So, it is better to name the scholars in the text, especially when they are used for the first time. Introduce your sources before you use their material.

> Matthiessen and Beach both argue that *The Ambassadors* is James's most accomplished novel, refuting Leavis's claim that it is a bad piece of fiction.

This is much clearer, and cuts out the need for the cumbersome references, making the sentence sound smoother and more authoritative. If you are using footnotes, you do not usually need to give a footnote unless you quote directly from a text (see pages 78–9, so name your sources as you go along, and remember to include them in your bibliography. However, if you are using Harvard style, you could also include the dates to avoid any confusion. This is especially helpful the first time a source is mentioned.

> Matthiessen (1944) and Beach (1954) both argue that *The Ambassadors* is James's most accomplished novel, refuting Leavis's claim (1948) that it is a poor piece of fiction.

Always acknowledge your sources actively. Do not rely on your footnotes and references to make your essay make sense. That is not their job. Make it absolutely clear who said what, and whether you and other scholars agree. Your essay will read much more coherently. Here are some more reasons to name your sources in the body of your text.

- **It sounds good:** Academics all enjoy a bit of name-dropping. Your tutor will be pleased if you flag up an idea put forward by an important scholar or cultural figure. Essays are all about showing what you have read and learned. Knowing about the key players in a debate is part of this. Besides, it is only polite to introduce people properly.

- **It helps your marker:** Remember that it is your job to make your essay accessible to the reader. Your marker may not have read all the books you refer to, so some help in sorting out who said what is often appreciated. For example, there have been thousands of books and articles published on Henry James since he wrote his novels. I would be surprised if anybody has read them all. Alternatively, your marker may have read all your secondary sources, in which case they will expect you to give credit to the scholar where it is due.

- **It makes for clarity:** One of the hardest skills in writing essays is making it crystal clear which ideas come from outside sources, which are based on common knowledge, and which are your own thoughts on the subject. Your marker will not know what your thoughts are, unless you make it clear where other people's ideas stop and yours start. Do not assume you can fudge this to your advantage. Your marker will probably assume that you have absorbed ideas from somewhere else unless you mark this out neatly.

- **It helps you avoid plagiarism:** If you keep track of who said what, and make this clear to your reader, you will never be in danger of plagiarism. There is more advice on this issue in the following chapter.

- **It helps with signposting:** Naming the scholar makes it easier to refer back to their idea further on in the essay. For example:

Later scholars such as Bradbury (1979) and Hutchison (2006) follow Matthiessen and Beach in opposing Leavis's view.

Keeping a firm grip on who voiced which idea will help you to hold your essay together and to construct a well-balanced piece of writing.

Ask yourself

- Is my essay about a text? Which one?
- Do my sources all agree with each other?
- Are any of my sources faulty?
- If I took my references out, would my essay still make sense?

Layout of quotations

It is important to present your quoted material neatly, so that your marker can see clearly where quotations start and stop. The rules for quoting primary and secondary material are the same. However, the format of your quote may vary depending on the length of the quote and the type of material you are quoting. The examples on the next few pages are referenced in MHRA style, but the layout of the material would be much the same in Harvard style. See Chapters 19 and 20 for more advice on referencing.

- **Short quotations.** Quotations of a few words should be incorporated into a sentence:

    ✓ Pip's 'great expectations' prove to be not at all what he imagines.

    or

    ✓ Joe's repeated phrase, 'what larks', represents his lack of education as well as his affectionate, boyish relationship with Pip. [2]

- **Quotations of up to 40 words.** These may also be incorporated into your text. They should be preceded by a colon or comma when appropriate:

    ✓ Charles Dickens sets Pip's story in a landscape similar to that of his own childhood: 'Ours was the marsh country, down by the river, within, as the river wound, twenty miles of the sea.'

The colon or comma is not needed if a word such as **that, which** or **whether** introduces the quotation. In this case, the quotation functions as a subordinate clause, and is an integral part of the wider sentence. When the quotation appears within a sentence, the final full stop should appear outside the quotation marks, even if the full stop is part of the original sentence. A page number in brackets should go inside the full stop when the quotation is run on in the text:

    ✓ Charles Dickens sets Pip's story in a landscape similar to that of his own childhood. Pip tells the reader that 'Ours was the marsh country, down by the river, within, as the river wound, twenty miles of the sea' (Dickens, p.1).

[2] Charles Dickens, *Great Expectations* (1861; repr. London: Everyman, 1994), p.193.

or

✓ Pip believes Miss Havisham is the source of his 'great expectations'.

- **Quotations of more than 40 words.** These should be set apart in an indented paragraph of their own. Leave a line, indent the whole paragraph one tab space from the margin, and set out the passage **without** quotation marks, except for those that may appear in the passage quoted:

✓ Charles Dickens sets Pip's story in a landscape similar to that of his own childhood. He quickly connects Pip's identity with this landscape and with the day on with he meets Magwitch:

> Ours was the marsh country, down by the river, within, as the river wound, twenty miles of the sea. My first most vivid and broad impression of the identity of things, seems to me to have been gained on a memorable raw afternoon towards evening. (Dickens, p.1)

Footnote numbers and subsequent page references in brackets should appear after the full stop for indented quotes. After an indented quote there is no need to indent the first line of text, unless you intend to start a new paragraph.

Quoting poetry

When quoting poetry, you should set it out as it appears in the original text. Check the punctuation carefully; it may not be as you expect. If you are quoting more than two lines, indent it and lay it out exactly as on the page. Give a footnote, as you would for prose, and include line numbers:

✓ My aspens dear, whose airy cages quelled,
Quelled or quenched in leaves the leaping sun,
All felled, felled, are all felled;

(Hopkins, p 76, 1–3)

If you are quoting up to two lines, run it on in the text like a short prose quote. Indicate line divisions with a slash:

✓ The speaker of 'Binsey Poplars' emphasises the fragility of nature by lamenting that 'only ten ot twelve'/Strokes of havoc unselve' the fallen trees (20–21). However, the form of Hopkins's poem restores order and beauty, through its own shape and pattern, and by its movement toward the 'Sweet especial rural scene' recalled in the final line (24).

Ellipses

To signal that you have omitted a short section of a quote, use ellipses in square brackets [...]. The brackets signal that these ellipses are yours:

✓ At such a time I found out for certain [...] that the low leaden line beyond was the river; and that the distant savage lair from which the wind was rushing, was the sea; and that the small bundle of shivers growing afraid of it all and beginning to cry, was Pip. (Dickens, p.1)

Make sure that the quote still makes grammatical sense in its own right. You must also make sure that you do not corrupt the sense of the author's original sentence. Only use ellipses to travel a short distance within a text. Use it to join sections of the same sentence, or possibly adjoining sentences. If you wish to quote clauses or phrases that are further apart, do so in two separate quotations. Do not use ellipses to indicate a large section of text which all seems relevant, but which you cannot be bothered to sift through for important phrases or sentences:

✗ Charles Dickens sets Pip's story in a landscape similar to that of his own childhood. He quickly connects Pip's identity with this landscape and with the day on with he meets Magwitch: 'My father's family [...] beginning to cry, was Pip' (Dickens, p.1).

Make quotations make sense

Every quote must be integrated into the grammar of the sentence or paragraph into which you wish to place it. Avoid dropping quotations into a sentence as though in brackets, like this:

✗ Pip, whose sister, 'I had cherished a profound conviction that her bringing me up by hand, gave her no right to bring me up by jerks' (Dickens, p.5), does not treat him well, has an unhappy childhood.

This does not make grammatical sense. The quotation simply lands in the middle of the sentence. This sentence would be better writen like this:

✓ Pip's older sister contributes to his unhappy childhood. Even as a small child, he is aware that her treatment of him is unfair. He recalls: 'I had cherished a profound conviction that her bringing me up by hand, gave her no right to bring me up by jerks' (Dickens, p.5).

Respect the text you are quoting. Take your time and use your sources carefully. Write something that reads well.

> **Top tip**
>
> Do not fill up your essay with lots of indented block quotes. Often one sentence or a key phrase will say just as much. Save your space for your own ideas.

> **Quick fix**
>
> - Use your sources to strengthen your argument. Name scholars in your work, so that your marker can see who said what. This helps your ideas to emerge more clearly.
> - You do not need to agree with everything that you read. An essay that has some sort of debate going on within it is much more interesting than a sequence of similar ideas or viewpoints. Use sources that contradict your viewpoint to give your work breadth.
> - Do not let your references get in the way of what you want to say. Make sure that your essay makes sense in its own right.
> - Lay out your quotations neatly. Anything under 40 words can be run into the text. Quotations of more than 40 words should be indented and set as a block.
> - Make sure that your quotations make sense. If you are quoting part of a sentence, make sure that you create a complete sentence that does not distort the original meaning of the quotation.

18

plagiarism

In this chapter you will learn:
- what plagiarism is and why it matters
- how you can avoid it.

What is plagiarism?

Plagiarism is viewed as a serious offence in the academic world and can lead to a student being thrown out of their college or university. There are many different forms of plagiarism, but the basic idea remains the same: **plagiarism is the use of the intellectual work of another person without due acknowledgement.** Academics do not just regard plagiarism as laziness or cheating. They see it as a form of stealing. Academics make their living by having ideas. If you use these ideas without giving credit for them, it is a bit like having a meal in a restaurant without paying. There are three main forms of plagiarism in student essays:

- quoting a source verbatim (word-for-word) without quotation marks as though you had written it yourself.
- using an idea which you have read, but failing to reference it, thus giving the impression that it was your own brilliant idea.
- copying the work of another student and submitting it as your own work.

None of these is allowed under any circumstances.

For students, these rules of plagiarism are in force to ensure that they really deserve the marks that they get for written work, and their final degree grade. These rules also apply to professional scholars and researchers as they write books and papers for publication. The consequences of plagiarism may be harsh for students, but the stakes are even higher for professional scholars. Jobs have been lost and reputations ruined for those who refused to follow the rules. However, none of this is necessary. Plagiarism is easy to avoid. Anyone who knows and follows the basic rules of referencing source material is unlikely to plagiarize by accident. This chapter sets out the basic principles of how and when to acknowledge other writers' work. The following two chapters provide the details of how to reference sources correctly.

Cut and paste chaos

Since the advent of the internet, most of us have become used to the idea that we can get any information we want, whenever we want it, and for any purpose we want at the touch of a button. We have also all become much better at cutting and pasting material from here and there to draw together lots of information in a hurry. However, if you still think you can write your academic essays like this, you had better go back and start reading this book all over again. A good essay is much more than a patchwork of sources tacked together. It should be a well thought-out argument which balances source materials with your own opinions and findings.

Remember that when you are writing an essay you are not just trying to reach the right answer, you are trying to show your marker the skills that you used to arrive at your answer, and the sources that helped you get there. A large part of this is being careful and transparent about all the sources that you use. All your information should be traceable back to a reliable source. Tutors are usually keen for students to explore interesting and unusual sources of information, but you must show where you found your information. Plagiarism is the deliberate failure to do this.

Show your sources

If you have copied something, even a short phrase, word-for-word out of a book, or if you have copied and pasted anything from an internet site, you must put it in quotation marks and give a reference. Changing one or two words, or paraphrasing a sentence does not release you from the obligation to name your sources. Look at the two versions of the same paragraph below. The first one is clearly plagiarizing. The second one shows where the ideas and the language really came from:

✗ Hamlet is reluctant to kill his uncle in revenge for his father's murder, but this may be connected to a repressed sexual attraction to his mother. So it is possible that his hesitancy is due to some special cause of repugnance for his task, even if he is unaware of the nature of this repugnance.

✓ Ernest Jones argues that Hamlet's reluctance to kill his uncle is connected to his own repressed sexual attraction to his mother. He claims that Hamlet's 'hesitancy' was due to 'some special cause of repugnance for his task', and that he was 'unaware of the nature of this repugnance' (Jones, 1910, p.84).

If you summarize someone else's argument, make sure that your marker can see what you are doing. Make sure that your own opinions and criticisms of your source material emerge distinctly as well. For example:

✓ Ernest Jones argues that Hamlet's reluctance to kill his uncle can all be traced back to his repressed desire for his mother. He claims that Hamlet's confusion about his feelings towards his father and his uncle are due to his jealousy at their relationships with Gertrude. However, this seems implausible, as Hamlet clearly loves and reveres his father, a detail which Jones fails to fit into his Freudian reading.

This make it clear which ideas are Jones's and which are the writer's.

> **Top tip**
>
> Students are more tempted to plagiarize when they have run out of time for an assignment. Organize your time well so that this will not happen to you.

Markers are smart

If you are ever tempted to cut a corner or two with a quick bit of quote-lifting, just remember this: your marker is quite smart. With a few rare exceptions, markers know more about the subject than you do, have a good idea of the kind of source material you might come across, and have seen a lot of essays at your level of work. They may also have a good idea of how capable you are and of the type of work which you are likely to submit. If there is something out of place about your essay, they will be on to it in a flash.

Many departments now ask students to submit essays electronically so that they can be processed through plagiarism-detecting software, which picks up any similarities to internet sources in unacknowledged source material. This software also stores each essay as it is processed, so that it can pick up similarities between students' essays. This is a formidable piece of marking weaponry.

However, a lot of plagiarists are caught because a tutor just gets a sense that something about the essay is not quite right. I once caught out two students who had cut and pasted material from the same internet source. I found myself reading almost identical paragraphs in two different essays. Some years ago at my university a student included in his essay several paragraphs of a book written by his tutor, and then submitted it as his own work for marking. He was apparently surprised to be caught.

Do not underestimate your marker. They can often tell if a phrase or a whole paragraph has been lifted from an outside source. They may have read the book or article in question just the day before marking your work. Many tutors are astute, sensitive readers with a keen sense of linguistic style and tone. It is difficult to fool them. If you can find something on the internet in five minutes, your marker can get a funny feeling about it and Google it just as fast. The stupid thing is that the effort required to plagiarize effectively is probably about the same amount of effort required to use the same sources in an argument and reference them properly. As I pointed out in Chapter 06, internet material can be unreliable and badly written, so it may not do your work any favours even if it does sneak through.

There will be information on avoiding plagiarism in your course guides, and on your college or university website. Every time you hand in an essay, you probably have to sign a declaration on the cover sheet saying that you have read and understood the rules of your institution. Make sure you have.

What about lectures?

Students often worry about how to incorporate information from lectures and seminars into their written work. Information given in a lecture becomes public knowledge. Feel free to use it in your work; that is what it is for. You can use your lecture notes to help you prepare your essay, but do not cite the lecture as though it were a text. Although lecturers are pleased to discover that you have been paying attention in class, they do not like to see their own phrases parroted back to them in written work. This makes them suspicious that you have not done much other reading on the subject. Be especially careful of this issue if English is not your first language. Sometimes, it can be hard to find alternative ways to express ideas when you are working in a second language. If this is the case, you need to work hard at your language skills. Find out if any extra help is available on campus.

If you can digest the information given in lectures and express it in your own words, your lecturer will feel that they have done a good job. However, you should try to interweave these ideas with research and reading that you have done while preparing for the assignment. Show that you have taken an interest in the topic and have developed your own ideas on it. If you want to use a quote from a class handout, look it up in the library, or email the lecturer and ask where you can find it. Do not cite the handout as though it were a published text. Do your own research and use it.

> **Ask yourself**
> - Is this my own idea?
> - Have I borrowed phrases from my sources?
> - Is it clear who said what?
> - Have I cited all my sources?

Collaboration

Universities and colleges exist so that students can learn together and share ideas. Lab work, field work and group projects often call for students to co-operate and work in a team. However, occasionally this goes too far, and co-operation turns in to collaboration. This is a difficult area to police. Most tutors will be delighted to overhear their students in the coffee bar or in the pub discussing what happened in the classroom earlier that day. However, they will not be pleased if they receive four pieces of written work that are essentially the same.

Be careful of this issue. Do not steal ideas from your classmates or work too closely with a friend on an assignment that is supposed to be an independent piece of work. If you have a study mate who keeps you company in the library, you might be wise to choose different topics for assignments, or to have a rule that you do not talk about the details of your work until you have finished writing. Be very wary of letting classmates read your work before it has been marked. If they copy your work, you could find yourself in trouble too.

If you want to ask someone to proofread your own work, try to find a friend who is taking a different course, and remember that you should ask them to correct only superficial errors, not to rewrite any of the content of the essay. They probably do not know as much about it as you do, anyway.

I thought of it first

If you have an inspired idea, only to find that some clever scholar got there first, do not panic. There are very few truly original ideas. The fact that someone else wrote it down and got it published shows that you are thinking along the right lines. Using this idea is not plagiarism, but the smart thing to do here is to present the idea as your point of view and to use the scholar to back you up. This will make you look better, not worse.

✓ Hamlet's relationships with women are all problematic. His supposed romance with Ophelia never demonstrates any shared affection or sexual attraction. He is unnaturally close to his mother, which complicates his relationship with his uncle, as Ernest Jones points out in his Freudian reading of the play.

This makes it clear that you have a strong opinion about Hamlet's romantic problems and have noticed this for yourself. However, it also makes clear that you are aware of Jones's similar idea. This makes you look intelligent and well-informed, which is exactly how you want to present yourself.

Quick fix

- Plagiarism is the use of the intellectual work of another person without due acknowledgement. Plagiarism can apply to printed material, internet material and the work of other students. It is a serious offence and can lead to you being thrown out of college or university.

- Learn how to give accurate references. Give a reference for any words that you quote directly from another text and for any source from which you use a significant idea. Do not borrow ideas from your friends and classmates. Do not let them borrow yours.

- Use internet sources with caution. Only use information from good sites. If you are not sure of what you have found, do not use it. Never cut and paste a section of text into your essay without using quotation marks and giving a reference.

- Citing sources will do more than keep you clear of the plagiarism rules. Showing where you found the ideas and contrasting these with your own views will make your essay stronger and more scholarly. It is much more likely to get a better mark this way.

19

referencing with author–date system

In this chapter you will learn:
- how to reference with the author–date system
- how to construct a reference list.

Why referencing matters

Good referencing demonstrates that you care about the accuracy and the reliability of your sources. It shows where your ideas come from, and it allows your reader to check up on the accuracy of your source material if required. It also shows that you are attentive to details, which gives your argument more authority. People will always be more willing to listen to your big ideas if you can get the small things right. So, referencing is a good chance to practise taking care with facts and figures: another skill that you will find useful in all sorts of contexts.

There are several kinds of referencing styles around. If you study more than one subject, you may be aware that different departments have different expectations about the ways you should reference your work. This can be very confusing, and you may receive conflicting advice from tutors in different subject areas. Some universities now have a blanket policy on style, insisting that all departments use the same system. Find out which style is standard for your subject or subjects and which style your tutors will expect to see. A good way to work out which style you should be using is to look at a couple of major journals in your subject area. Journals sometimes have styles of their own, but mostly they follow one of a handful of standard systems. Journal websites usually have a 'notes for contributors' or a 'style guide' page. These webpages can be excellent places to look for good advice about referencing practices within your subject area.

Which style?

Although there are many variations in referencing style, most systems fall into one of two categories.

Author–date

The most common style of referencing is the author–date system. This is used in science and social science subjects, and in some arts and humanities subjects. This is often referred to as the Harvard system, as one version of it originated at Harvard University. The author–date system is also closely related to the style systems of the Modern Language Association (MLA) and the American Psychological Association (APA). In the author–date system, a reference list of works which have been cited is given at the end of the essay. Each time information is used from one of these works, the writer of the essay provides the following information in brackets in the text: the name of the author, the date of the book or article used, and the relevant page number. The reader of the essay can flip to the end of the essay to check for more information if necessary.

Footnotes

The other dominant system of referencing relies on footnotes. This system is more frequently used in arts and humanities subjects, as it is particularly well-suited to projects dealing with a lot of textual material. In the UK the standard version of this is MHRA style. The letters stand for the Modern Humanities Research Association, which publishes a useful style guide explaining this system. In the US, this system is usually known as Chicago style, as this is the style used by The University of Chicago Press. There are minor variations, but the ground rules of these systems are the same. The first time a source is cited a footnote is given, which provides all the necessary bibliographic information. On subsequent references, the author's name or a short reference and page number are given in brackets in the text. At the end of the essay or article, a bibliography is given, listing all the works cited or consulted.

This chapter will show you the basics of how to use the author–date system. It will explain how to incorporate quotations into your text using bracketed references. It will also show you how to construct a reference list. Chapter 20 will show you how to use the MHRA system. It will explain how to incorporate quotations into your text using footnotes. It will also show you how to construct a bibliography. However, the advice here is very basic, and there is room for only a few examples. You would be wise to invest in a style guide for whichever referencing style you will use throughout your studies.

Using the author–date system

The author–date system is an excellent referencing system to use if your subject calls for a thorough knowledge of recent scholarly publications such as journal articles. This style makes it easy to refer to relevant scholarship in your text, even if you have not quoted it directly. It also makes the publication date of this scholarship very visible, which is often important. However, every system has its drawbacks.

When you are using the author–date system, your text can fill up with a lot of bracketed material. Try to ensure that this does not spoil the flow of your argument. There is also a danger with this style that you will just tuck a reference into a sentence without quite making it clear exactly which ideas or phrases are derived from your cited material. Try to be as specific as possible about this. Talk about your authors in your text, to make it clear who said what. Make sure that your text reads well and makes sense in its own right. References are there to show where your ideas came from. They should not be used to glue your argument together. See Chapter 17 for some more advice on this issue.

Top tip

Find out if your department has a referencing style sheet which you should follow. Ask your tutor which style of referencing they want to see in your work.

References in the text

When you quote material from a source or when you refer to an argument or information from an article or book, you should give an author–date reference in brackets in the main body of your text. Try to place this reference close to the relevant material without spoiling the shape of your sentence. References should be given in the following format:

(Author's surname, date of publication). For example:

   (Bernard, 2000)

This is the same whether you are dealing with a book, an article or some other kind of source. If there are two authors, give both surnames:

   (Akroyd and Hughes, 1992)

If there are more than two, give the first name then add, *et al.* in italics:

   (Cloke *et al.*, 2004)

If you have quoted directly from the text, you should also give a page number:

   (Smith, 1983, p.6)

If you use the author's name in the text, you only need to give the date. Here is an example of a paragraph which includes several author–date references:

> Quantitative researchers have in the past been caricatured as 'number-crunchers' (Smith, 1983, p.6). However, in recent years, more mixed-method approaches have developed in social-science research. For example, researchers using surveying techniques recognize the importance of social interaction as part of the survey process (Bernard, 2000), while researchers using ethnographic approaches are also learning to adopt statistical and inductive methods (Cloke *et al.*, 2004). Ackroyd and Hughes (1992) point out that whatever methods are used, the research should always be systematic and rigorous.

Remember to use quotation marks for significant words and phrases which you have lifted directly from your source material.

If you have two items on your list published by the same author in the same year, then mark these **a, b, c,** etc. in the reference list. You can then refer to these clearly in the text:

(Bernard, 2000a)
(Bernard, 2000b)

Secondary references

If you wish to make use of material which was a quotation within one of your source items, make it clear in the text that this is what you are doing. This is called secondary referencing. Give author–date information for both texts, and use the phrase 'cited in' to show where you found your information:

> Ackroyd and Hughes (1992) call for systematic and rigorous research (cited in Hutchison, 2007).

Secondary referencing is permissible. However, try not to use this too often. Your marker will become suspicious that you have not read very widely if you quote a lot of second-hand material. If possible, track down the original article and read it too. You can then give a direct reference. This article is also likely to be relevant to your topic, so it should be worth reading.

Reference lists

At the end of the essay you should include a reference list, sometimes called a 'works-cited' list, which contains the full bibliographic references to all of your sources. You can divide this into primary and secondary sources, if appropriate. However, you should not create separate sections for books, journals, or other types of source material. Present your list in alphabetical order of the author's surname. The author's name and initials should be reversed to make this order clear. If there are two authors, place the item in the list according to the surname of the first author. You should also reverse the name and initials of all the authors. The format of the reference will vary slightly depending of the type of publication. Take special care to get the punctuation right.

Books

Put book titles in italics or underline them. Whichever you choose, you should be consistent. List books using the following format: author (date) *title of book in italics*. Place of publication: publisher. For example:

> Bernard, H. R. (2000) *Social Research Methods: Qualitative and Quantitative Approaches*. London: Sage Publications.

If you do not know where to find this information, open the cover of your book and turn over one or two pages. On the left-hand page opposite the title page, or behind the title page, you will see some small type, which you have possibly never stopped to look at before. This page gives you the publication history of the text. Here you should find the three pieces of information you need to complete the reference: place of publication, publisher and date. Sometimes these also appear on the title page. If several places of publication appear, give the city closest to where you are. This is probably where the book in your hand was printed, and sometimes there are differences between the different national editions of a text.

If a book has two or more authors, list all of these as they appear in the book. Remember to reverse the name and initial of each of the authors:

> Ackroyd, S. and Hughes, J. A. (1992) *Data Collection in Context*. London: Longman.

Cloke, P., Cook, I., Crang, P., Goodwin, M., Painter, J. and Philo, C. (2004) *Practising Human Geography*. London: Sage Publications.

Translated books should give both author and translator:

Derrida, J. (1978) *Writing and Difference*. (A. Bass. Trans.) Chicago: University of Chicago Press. (Original work published 1967.)

Chapters in edited books

Titles of chapters or articles in edited books should be given in quotation marks. When you reference a book chapter in the text, give the name of the author of the chapter and the publication date. In the reference list, cite the chapter first, followed by the reference information for the book. The name of an editor or translator is not reversed: Author of article (date) 'title of article'. *In* editor of book, ed. *Title of Book*. Place of publication: publisher, pp.page numbers of article. For example:

Conklin, H. C. (1968) 'Ethnography'. *In* D. L. Sills, ed. *International Encyclopedia of the Social Sciences*. New York: Macmillan, pp.172–8.

A reference to a conference paper published in conference proceedings should follow the format for a chapter in an edited book. The date and place of the conference should be given after the title of the conference proceedings.

Articles in journals

Titles of articles should also be given in quotation marks. Titles of journals are given in italics like book titles. Give the information for the article, followed by the information for the journal: author (date) 'title of article in quotation marks'. *Title of journal in italics*, volume no., (part volume no.), pp.page numbers of article.

Smith, J. K. (1983) 'Quantitative Versus Qualitative Research: An Attempt to Clarify the Issue'. *Educational Researcher*, 12 (3), pp.6–13.

Some users of the author–date system omit the quotation marks, but these are useful because they clarify where the title of the article ends and the journal title begins. However, if your tutor strikes them out, do not argue about it. Give the title of the article in full, even if it is a long one. Always list all the authors. For example:

> Pettitt, J., Crombie, C., Schümperli, D. and Müller B. (2002) 'The *Caenorhabditis elegans* histone hairpin-binding protein is required for core histone expression and is essential for embryonic and postembryonic cell division'. *Journal of Cell Science*, 115, pp.857–66.

Electronic journals

Online journals should be cited in the same format as print journals. However, you should also add the url address of the article and the date on which you accessed the article: author (date), 'title of article'. *Title of journal*, volume number (and part), pp.pages numbers. url [accessed date]. For example:

> Van Wienen, M. (1995) 'Poetics of the Frugal Housewife: A Modernist Narrative of the Great War and America'. *American Literary History*, 7 (1), pp.55–91. http://links. jstor.org/sici?sici=08967148%28199521%297%3A1%3C5 5%3APOTFHA%3E2.0.CO%3B2-K [Accessed 10 August 2007].

Some online journal articles now have a Digital Object Identifier (DOI), which is like a digital barcode or serial number for electronic data. If you have accessed the article online, you should also quote this DOI and give the date when you read the article. Many online journals provide a model of how the journal material should be cited. This is a good sign as it suggests that you have found a reputable academic source, which expects you to reference it properly. If this is the case, reproduce the style given on the website:

> Pettitt, J. (2005). The cadherin superfamily (December 29, 2005), WormBook, ed. The *C. elegans* Research Community, Wormbook, doi/10.1895/wormbook.1.50.1, http://www. wormbook.org/ [Accessed 10 August 2007].

Websites

If you are referencing online material that is not published as a journal article, you should give as much of the following information as you can find: author (date), 'title of article'. *Title of web publication.* Edition. Date of publication. Place of publication: publisher. [Accessed date].

> Cornwall, N. (2006), 'The Aspern Papers'. *The Literary Encyclopedia.* 17 Jan 2006. The Literary Dictionary Company. http://www.litencyc.com/php/sworks.php?rec=true&UID=1559 [accessed 10 August 2007].

Websites vary in the amount of information they give. However, reliable websites usually make this information easily available. If you cannot find any of this information, you should ask yourself whether the website is a usable academic source. You will find some of this information very hard to find on big internet encyclopedias such as Wikipedia and Questia. Remember that the point of giving references is to ensure that your information is reliable and traceable. If you cannot do this, you should think twice about using it.

Newspaper articles

Cite newspaper and magazine articles in a format similar to journal articles: Author (date) 'title of article'. *Title of newspaper*, date of publication. p.no. For example:

> Elliot, L. and Wintour, P. (2007) 'Bush agrees to CO2 cut, with strings attached'. *The Guardian*, 8 June 2007, p.2.

Films

Film, TV and other media should be referenced in the following format: *Title of film in italics* (date of release). Type of material. Director or equivalent. Place of production: distributor. For example:

> *The Grapes of Wrath* (1940). Film. Directed by John Ford. USA: Twentieth Century Fox.

Graphs and charts

Graphs and charts should be referenced as carefully as textual material. Give a reference immediately under the graph, naming the source of your information (see pages 94 and 96). List the document in which you found this information in the reference list. If you have used more than one source in compiling your own graph or chart, then cite both of these in the bracketed reference and cite these separately in the reference list, for example:

> Office of National Statistics (1999) *Key population and Vital Statistics, Local and Health Authority Areas*. London: Stationary Office.

> General Register Office Scotland (2000) *2000-Based Population projections for Scottish Areas*. http://www/gro-scotland. gov.uk/grosweb.nsf/pages/

Maps, illustrations and works of art

Maps taken from a published source should be cited in the same format as textual material. However, you should also add in the scale of the map:

> Ordnance Survey (2004) *Ballater and Glen Clova* 44, 1:50 000. Southampton: Ordnance Survey.

Book illustrations or pictures reproduced in a book follow a format similar to that of chapters or articles in books. Give the name of the illustrator or artist, the title of the illustration or picture and then the details of the book. Note that the name of the artist is given in full, not initialized:

> Stone, Marcus. 'With Estella After All'. *In* C. Dickens (1994) *Great Expectations*. London: Everyman (originally published 1861).

Pictures, photographs and other works of art in public galleries are referenced by their location. It is also standard practice to state the medium:

> Holbein, Hans (1533) *The Ambassadors*. [Painting]. London: National Gallery.

Literary texts

Literary texts follow similar formats to those given above. Novels should be cited as books. Short stories in anthologies follow the format given for an article or chapter in an edited book. Short-story titles go in quotation marks. Plays follow the format for single-author books unless the play is published in a collection or anthology, in which case it also follows the format for a chapter in an edited book. Titles of plays go in italics.

Titles of short poems appear in quotations marks. Do not cite a poem as a separate item in a reference list. Give a reference to the collection of poems or anthology. A long poem, which was originally published as a volume in its own right, such as *Paradise Lost* or *In Memoriam*, should follow the format for a single-author book, unless it is included in an edited volume.

Quick fix

- Find out if the author–date system is standard for your subject. Look at a few journals in your field to see what other scholars do. Ask if there is a style sheet for your department or college.
- Pay attention to the punctuation in your reference list entries. Try to be consistent with this. Markers are always impressed by attention to detail.
- Construct your reference list as you write your essay. It will save time and you will be less likely to leave anything out.
- Reference internet sources as accurately as books and printed journal articles. Use DOI numbers where these are available.

20
referencing
with footnotes

In this chapter you will learn:
- how to reference with footnotes
- how to construct a bibliography.

Footnotes are an excellent way of referencing material if your subject involves working closely with textual material. There are several benefits of this system: full bibliographic information is available to the reader as the essay unfolds, not just at the end; there are fewer brackets cluttering up your sentences; and a bibliography provides a comprehensive list of all sources consulted. On the down side, this form of referencing is quite labour-intensive. Some information is given twice, and your footnotes can eat in to your word limit.

The following pages give advice on the MHRA system, which is based on footnotes. The first time you mention a text, give a footnote. See below for the correct format. If you mention the same text later in your essay, do not give a footnote. Give a short reference in brackets within your text: (Dickens, p.67). If you are using more than one text by the same author it might be less confusing to give a short version of the title or an abbreviation: (*Great Ex,* p.67) or (*GE,* p.67).

Here are a few things to avoid when using footnotes:

- Do not use footnotes for extra information that you would like to include but cannot fit into your essay. If the information does not earn its place in your text, then leave it out.

- Do not footnote your title, even if it includes a complicated term or the title of a book. Wait until you get into your essay before you start giving references.

- Do not use *ibid* or *op. cit.* Few people really understand how to compose or read these properly, so they are just confusing.

- Do not put more than one footnote number in a sentence. If you have more than one quotation in a sentence, give both references in the same footnote in the order in which they appear in the sentence. Always place the footnote number at the end of the sentence.

- Do not put a footnote number before quotation marks, a question mark or a full stop. A footnote reference number should follow all punctuation.

At the end of your essay you should also include a bibliography. The format is slightly different for books, articles and websites. The rules are given below. Make sure you copy the punctuation as well. Footnotes should always have a full stop.

Books

On first reference to a book, you should give a footnote in the following format: author's name, *title of book in italics* (place of publication: publisher, date), p.no.

Rules for primary and secondary sources are the same:

> Bella Bathurst, *The Lighthouse Stevensons* (London: Harper Collins, 2000), p.23.

> Vladimir Nabokov, *Lolita* (1959; repr. London: Penguin, 2000), p.47.

> F. O. Matthiessen, ed., *The Oxford Book of American Verse* (New York: Oxford University Press, 1950), p.556.

> Robert Frost, *The Poetry of Robert Frost*, ed. by Edward Connery Lathem (London: Cape, 1971; repr. 2001), p.105.

Translated books should give both author and translator:

> Jacques Derrida, *Writing and Difference* (1967), trans. by A. Bass (Chicago: University of Chicago Press, 1978), p.24.

If you do not know where to find the necessary publication information, see page 179 in the previous chapter. If the text is a reprint, give both the date of the original publication and the date of the reprint. This will probably mean the oldest and most recent dates you can find at the start of the book. See the Nabokov and Derrida examples above. If you are using a collected edition, give both the author's name and the editor's name. See the Frost reference above. It is only necessary to give an edition number if the content is likely to differ significantly between editions. This is often the case for reference books, scientific textbooks and collections of poetry.

Articles or essays in books

Titles of articles or essays are placed in quotation marks to indicate that they are not book titles. Give the details of the article, followed by the details of the book in which it appears, including the editor, if there is one. Give the page numbers for the complete article, followed by the page number for your quotation: author's name, 'title of article', in *title of book*, ed. by editor's name (Place: publisher, date), page numbers, p.no.

For example:

> Philip Horne, 'Henry James and the Invention of Novel Theory', in *The Cambridge Companion to Henry James*, ed. by Jonathan Freedman (Cambridge: Cambridge University Press, 1998), 79–101, p.85.

If you wish to quote from an excerpt reprinted in a collection of source material, give as much information as you can find about the original text, followed by the information about the book you are using. This information should be available in the footnotes or bibliography:

> M. Eastwood, 'The New Woman in Fiction and in Fact', *Humanitarian*, 5 (1894), 375–9; repr. in *The Fin de Siecle: A Reader in Cultural History c.1880–1900*, ed. by Sally Ledger and Roger Luckhurst (Oxford: Oxford University Press, 2000), 90–92, p.90.

Articles in journals

These follow a similar format, but the information about editor, place of publication and publisher is not necessary. The title of the article appears in quotation marks. The title of the journal or newspaper appears in italics. For journals, give the issue number followed by the year: author's name, 'title of article', *title of journal*, volume number (date), page numbers, p.no.

> Lorna J. Philip, 'Planned Villages in South-West Scotland, 1730–1855; Analysing Functional Characteristics', *Landscapes*, 6 (1), 83–107, p.101.

> T. S. Eliot, 'In Memory of Henry James', *Egoist*, 5 (1918), 1-2, p.2.

Websites

Give as much of the following information as you can find: author, 'title of article', place of publication: publisher, (date) [accessed date].

> S. N. Clark, 'Virginia Woolf: A Short Biography', Virginia Woolf Society of Great Britain, (2000). http://orlando.jp.org/VWSGB/dat/vwbiog.html [accessed 23 August 2007].

As I noted in the previous chapter, reliable websites usually make publication information easily available. If you cannot find any of this information, ask yourself whether the website is a suitable source. Avoid study-notes sites and big online encyclopedias such as Wikipedia and Questia where you cannot find out who wrote what you are reading. Remember that the point of giving references is to ensure that your information is reliable and traceable. If you cannot do this, avoid using it.

Short stories

As with essays and articles, short-story titles are placed in quotation marks to indicate that they are not book titles. Give the details of the short story, followed by the details of the book in which it appears, including the editor, if there is one. Give the page numbers for the complete story, followed by the page number for your quotation: author's name, 'title of short story', in *title of book*, ed. by editor's name (place: publisher, date), page numbers, p.no.

If the story has been reprinted in an anthology, you should also give the original date of the story if you can find it: author's name, 'Title of short story' (original date); repr. in *title of anthology*, ed. by Editor's name (Place: publisher, date), page numbers, p.no.

Vernon Lee, 'Winthrop's Adventure', in *The Virago Book of Victorian Ghost Stories*, ed. by Richard Dalby (London: Virago, 1988), 105–34, p.127.

Ernest Hemingway, 'A Pursuit Race', in *Men Without Women* (1928; repr. London: Arrow, 1994) 111–15, p.113.

Willa Cather, 'A Death in the Desert' (1905); repr. in *The Oxford Book of American Short Stories*, ed. by Joyce Carol Oates (Oxford: Oxford University Press, 1994), 264–84, p.275.

Plays

Play titles appear in italics. For a first footnote give a reference to the edition or collection used:

> William Shakespeare, *Hamlet*, in *The Complete Works of Shakespeare*, 2 vols (New York: Nelson Doubleday, 1968), vol II, Act II, Sc. 2, p.611.

> Brian Friel, *Philadelphia, Here I Come* (London: Faber, 1965), p.42.

For subsequent references give an abbreviated version of the title, if necessary, followed by act, scene and line numbers, if you have these. For a modern play which has undivided acts, it often makes more sense to give page numbers instead:

> (*Hamlet*, III.1.24–34)

or

> (*Philadelphia*, p.93)

Poetry

Titles of short poems appear in quotations marks. It is not usually necessary to cite a poem as a separate item in a footnote. Give a reference to the collection of poems or anthology and the page number. The exception to this rule would be a very long poem which was originally published as a volume in its own right, such as *Paradise Lost* or *In Memoriam*. This should follow the format for a play title as above. For subsequent references to a poem, give line numbers rather than page numbers.

Newspaper articles

Cite newspaper and magazine articles in a format similar to journal articles:

> author, 'title of article', *title of newspaper*, date of publication, p.no. For example:

> Larry Elliot and Patrick Wintour, 'Bush agrees to CO2 cut, with strings attached', *The Guardian*, 8 June 2007, p.2.

> Iain Sinclair, 'Silence on the Euston Road', *London Review of Books*, 18 August 2005, 14–16, p.15.

Films

Information in film references is separated by full points rather than commas: *Title of film*. Director's name. Distributor. Date. For example:

> *The Grapes of Wrath*. Dir. John Ford. Twentieth Century Fox, 1940.

Graphs and charts

The same rules apply for referencing graphs and charts in MHRA style as in Harvard. Give a reference immediately under the graph naming the source of your information (see pages 94 and 96). List the document in which you found this information in your footnote and bibliography. If you have used more than one source in compiling your own graph or chart then cite both of these in the footnote and cite these separately in the bibliography.

> Office of National Statistics, *Key population and Vital Statistics, Local and Health Authority Areas* (London: Stationary Office, 1999), p.22.

> General Register Office Scotland *2000-Based Population projections for Scottish Areas* (2000). http://www/gro-scotland.gov.uk/grosweb.nsf/pages/ [accessed, 14 June 2007]

Maps, illustrations and works of art do not require footnotes if they are clearly captioned. Include the relevant reference material in the caption. Then, give another full reference in the bibliography. Appropriate styles are listed below on page 193.

Secondary references

Try to avoid giving secondary references. You should normally only quote material which you have actually seen. If you want to use material quoted in someone else's work, look it up. If you cannot find it, and really want or need to use the quote, make sure the original author's name appears in the text when you use their material. Begin the footnote 'Quoted in'. Thereafter, give the publication details of the book or article in which you found the material. Cite the book or article, not the quote, in your bibliography.

Bibliography

At the end of every essay give a bibliography. List works from which you have quoted or which have informed your thinking, even if you have only used one or two texts. Do not list works which you have not read or which you glanced at briefly. If you are working on a project which involved primary source material, divide the bibliography into primary texts and secondary texts. See Chapter 17 if you are unsure which is which. In MHRA style, references in a bibliography follow the same format as footnotes with two exceptions:

- The surname of the author is placed first, so that the items can easily be put into alphabetical order.
- A bibliographic reference does not have a full stop.

If you have quoted several essays from a collection in the course of your essay, you can simply list the collected edition in the bibliography. Use a long dash to signal more than one text by a writer.

Here is a short sample bibliography for an essay on two novels by Virginia Woolf:

Primary texts:

Woolf, Virginia, *Mrs Dalloway* (1925; repr. Oxford: Oxford Classics, 1998)
   – *To the Lighthouse* (1927; repr. London: Grafton, 1987)

Secondary texts:

Bowlby, Rachel, *Virginia Woolf: Feminist Destinations* (Oxford: Blackwell, 1988)

Clark, S. N. 'Virginia Woolf: A Short Biography', Virginia Woolf Society of Great Britain, (2000). http://orlando.jp.org/VWSGB/dat/vwbiog.html [Accessed 23 August 2007].

Gaipa, Mark, 'An Agnostic's Daughter's Apology: Materialism, Spiritualism, and Ancestry in Woolf's *To the Lighthouse*', *Journal of Modern Literature*, 26 (2), (2003), 1–41

Lee, Hermione, *The Novels of Virginia Woolf* (London: Methuen, 1977)

McNeillie, Andrew (ed.), *The Essays of Virginia Woolf*, 5 vols (London: Hogarth Press, 1987), vol II

If there is more than one author or editor, list them in the order in which they appear in the book. Only reverse the name of the first contributor. The lists of further reading at the end of each section of this book are set out in MHRA bibliography form. See these for more examples.

Top tip

Build up your bibliography as you write your essay. You will be less likely to leave anything out. Remember to include texts which influenced your thinking, even if you do not quote from them directly.

Maps, illustrations and works of art

Maps taken from a published source should be listed in the same format as textual material. However, you should also add in the scale of the map:

> Ordnance Survey, *Ballater and Glen Clova* 44, 1:50 000. (Southampton: Ordnance Survey, 2004)

Book illustrations or pictures reproduced in a book follow a format similar to that for chapters or articles in books. Give the name of the illustrator or artist, the title of an illustration or picture and then the details of the book:

> Stone, Marcus, 'With Estella After All'. *In* Charles Dickens, *Great Expectations*, (1861; repr. London: Everyman, 1994)

Pictures, photographs and other works of art in public galleries are referenced by their location. Include the date, if it is available:

> Holbein, Hans, *The Ambassadors* (1533), London: National Gallery

If you have a lot of illustrations in a large piece of work such as a dissertation, it is a good idea to include a list of illustrations at the beginning next to the contents page. Set this out in the same style as the picture references in your bibliography.

Chicago and Vancouver

MHRA style is very similar to Chicago style, used in the US. The basic format for footnotes is almost identical. The format for the bibliography differs slightly in that full stops are used to divide information, rather than commas and brackets. For example:

> Lee, Hermione. *The Novels of Virginia Woolf*. London: Methuen, 1977.

In Vancouver style, often used in medical journals, subsequent references to a text give the number of the footnote in which the text is first cited, followed by a page number. This system is very economical with space, but can be difficult to use well. Most medical schools prefer the author–date system for student assignments.

Quick fix

- Give a footnote the first time you need to reference a text. Always put the footnote number at the end of the sentence. If you mention the same text or quote from it later in your essay, give a short reference in brackets.

- Avoid using footnotes for extra information. Work this into your essay if possible. If it really does not fit into the body of your argument, you should probably leave it out.

- Avoid using secondary references. Try not to use any material which you have not actually seen for yourself.

- Give a bibliography, even if you only have one or two books to list. It looks professional and is a good habit to form. List anything you have quoted and anything relevant which you read while you were preparing your essay.

Try it out: Using sources

Plagiarism exercise

Read the following passage from a journal article about the growth of telephone and telegraph technology in the US in the late nineteenth century. Then read the essay extract below. As it stands, this extract plagiarizes heavily from the journal article. Rewrite the essay extract so that it makes legitimate use of the article and gives appropriate credit to its author.

Journal extract

Few features of late-nineteenth-century life seemed more novel or remarkable to observers than the technologies of action at a distance. Chief among these were the railroad, telegraph, and telephone. In the decades after the Civil War, American railroads linked the corners of the continent with thousands of miles of track. The Western Union Telegraph Company, one of the United States' first nation-spanning corporate monopolies, completed a transcontinental telegraph line in 1861, providing theoretically instantaneous communication from coast to coast. And the telephone, born in the centennial year of 1876, rapidly grew to eclipse the telegraph, promising to connect every home and every life to new national networks of communication and exchange.

Robert MacDougall, 'The Wire Devils: Pulp Thrillers, the Telephone, and Action at a Distance in the Wiring of a Nation', *American Quarterly*, 58 (3), 2007, 715–41, p.716.

Essay extract

American society in the second half of the nineteenth century was troubled by the possibility of action at a distance which new technologies made possible. Chief among these were the telephone, the telegraph and the railroad. In the decades after the Civil War, American railroads linked the corners of the continent with thousands of miles of track. Starting in 1861, telegraph companies also began to span the nation, providing instantaneous communication from coast to coast. After 1876, the telephone quickly eclipsed the telegraph, creating new national networks of communication.

Referencing exercise

1 Write a reference list of the following texts using the author–date system.

2 Write a bibliography of the same texts using the MHRA system.

Charles Darwin: Voyaging by Janet Brown, 1995, London, Jonathan Cape

Ben Marsden and Crosbie Smith, 'Engineering Empires – A Cultural History of Technology in Nineteenth-Century Britain', Palgrave, London: 2005.

Victorian Studies, Vol 49: No 2. (2007) pages 218–28. 'Imaging Interiority: Photography, Psychology, and Lyric Poetry', Laura Mandell.

19th Century Science: An Anthology, edited by A.S.Weber, Broadview Press, Peterborough, Ontario. 2000

Emile Zola, *La Bête Humaine*, translated by Roger Pearson, Oxford World's Classics, Oxford University Press, 1996, first published, 1890.

Herbert Horz, Philosophical Concepts of Space and Time, in Einstein a Centenary Volume, edited by A.P. French: Heinemann, London 1979, 229–41.

Answers can be found on pags 202–3.

Conclusion

This book has given you the key skills you need to tackle any piece of written work.

Of course, there is still more that you can learn and, as you apply what you have read in these pages, you will create your own strategies for handling problem areas in your own subject. As you develop your skills, remember a few basic principles:

- **Think big.** Think about the skills you are acquiring, the degree you are taking and the subject you are studying. Learn to see your written work as part of the broader process of your education in a wide and fascinating subject.
- **Pay attention to details.** Take care with the little elements of language and layout that are easy to overlook. Attention to detail is the sign of a thorough and hard-working mind. It is a very good habit to form, and can help you develop into a more precise thinker.

- **Make life easy for your marker.** Always remember that essays look rather different when you have a pile of 20 to mark for the following day. Give your marker something that is neatly presented and a pleasure to read. It can only help.
- **Enjoy what you write.** Studying should not be a chore. Learn to love the language, and use it with focus and style.

You will never regret the time you spend learning to write well. It is a skill that you will find useful for the rest of your life.

try it out: answers

Part One: Where do I start?

What kind of assignment is each of the following questions: formal essay, literature review, project report, learning log, case study or close reading?

1 learning log
2 formal essay
3 close reading
4 case study
5 project report
6 literature review
7 formal essay

Are the following questions broad or focused? Are there any that are basically focused, but have an element which requires clarification?

1 Focused – Although marriage and money are broad themes, keeping these within the boundaries of one novel creates a tight, direct question.
2 Focused – A reasoned argument will be focused and well supported by evidence, even if the topic ranges broadly.
3 Broad and focused – The first half of this question is very broad. However, the demand for specific examples and maps, diagrams and data will make this more focused. Choose your examples carefully to support your argument.
4 Broad – Africa is a big continent. This question needs to focus in on specific countries or regions to become manageable. It would work better if the final section read, 'Discuss with reference to Kenya and Tanzania.'

5 Very broad – This question covers 200 years. Think carefully about whether you could focus on a shorter period of time within this period or limit the question in some other way. Seek clarification from your tutor if you are in doubt about what this question is asking.

6 Focused – A quotation question often appears to invite a general discussion. However, you should address the specific issues raised by the quotation and how controversial these may be. You should also think about the significance of the identity of the speaker.

Part Two: Building your answer

What is wrong with the reasoning in the following extracts?

1 **Hamlet's indecision leads to his own tragic death and the death of innocent bystanders such as Polonius, Ophelia and Laertes. Therefore, Shakespeare's play shows that indecision is the cause of tragedy. Hamlet should have killed Claudius sooner.**

This extract jumps to a hasty conclusion based on a narrow view of the evidence. Hamlet's indecision is only one causal factor within a complex plot. This line of reasoning fails to account for Hamlet's noble reluctance to spill blood, his doubts about whether the ghost of his father can be trusted, and Claudius's plot to poison Hamlet, which causes the deaths of Laertes and Gertrude.

2 **Because primary-school children are naturally reluctant to learn, teachers need to develop strategies to engage their attention and encourage effort in the classroom.**

The extract has a false premise. Young children are naturally keen to learn, but can be alienated from the learning process in school by a range of factors. Teachers do need to develop creative learning strategies, but not for the reason given here.

3 **Poor essays often contain many surface errors. Students who read quickly are prone to missing surface errors when they check their work. Therefore, students who read quickly generally write poor essays.**

This extract does have a certain amount of logic, but does not quite add up, because it does not cover enough instances to prove the point. It will not always be the case that a quick reader will miss surface errors. Besides, an essay is not graded solely on whether it contains surface errors. Quick readers may get through more source material and develop a stronger grasp of the issue at stake in the essay. So reading quickly is not the cause of poor essays, but may sometimes be connected with it. Therefore this argument is not sufficient.

4 **In the 1840s and 50s, many miles of railway track were laid and more people began to travel by train. In these decades, sales of fiction also rose dramatically. From this it is possible to deduce that sales of fiction increased because many people were buying novels to read on long train journeys.**

This argument assumes an element of cause between two statements which are associated or correlated by some other type of connection. In this case the two statements are linked by historical period, but just because two things happen around about the same time does not mean that one must have caused the other. This is called a false correlation. There is, in fact, a link between the two statements, but this argument pinpoints the link wrongly. In the 1840s and 50s railways and printing presses were powered by steam, and as steam technology developed both railway travel and printed material became affordable to a wider section of the public. So these elements were linked by a common cause, but one element did not cause the other.

Editing your work: Find the surface errors in the following extracts.

Corrections are marked in bold.

1 If **exercise** cannot prevent coronary heart disease (CHD), one must ask whether **exercise** can lessen the risk of **CHD**. **However, physical** activity is only one possible primary preventive measure. **Other** preventive measures include **giving** up smoking, lowering blood pressure and a lowering of serum total **cholestorol**.

2 Since independence, Kenya has **ensured** a rapid expansion in the numbers of traders and **bureaucrats** by a process of legislation and **licensing**: e.g. the Trades **Licensing** Act of **1967**. The government also saw to it that the fertile 'White Highlands' were distributed among settlements in schemes such as the Million **Acres** Scheme. The point behind such provision was capitalist in **principle**.

3 Hamlet is **a** famously complex play – **complex** and difficult to understand in the sense that at the end of the tragedy many questions are left **un**answered. Hamlet is not a typical tragic hero, **although** the character of **Hamlet** can be interpreted in many different ways.

4 Mixing **quantitative** and qualitative methods **provides** more valid and reliable results. **There** are two fundamental questions to be asked by the researcher when considering using the mixed method; firstly, what is the most suitable data collection method; and **secondly**, how can the data be most effectively **combined** or integrated?

Part Three: Using language

Put the apostrophes in the correct places in the following sentences:

1 It's time that the cat had its dinner.
2 They're getting the ship ready for its first voyage.
3 He's so tall he'll bang his head if he doesn't watch out.
4 It's a pity that James's sister can't come to the children's party.
5 We've asked Caroline's brother to find out who's coming.

Use commas, semi-colons and colons to mark the clauses in these sentences so that they make sense:

1 Not only is it damp and cold; it is also dark.
2 However difficult it seems at first, driving a car, like riding a bicycle, soon becomes second nature.
3 However, you require a lot of practice, which can take a long time.
4 The books which were on the shelf had not been read.
   or
   The books, which were on the shelf, had not been read.
5 There are three things you need to do: clean out the fireplace; lay a new fire with wood, coal, paper and firelighters; and light it with the matches.

Add capitals and punctuation to the following paragraph.

Brooklyn Bridge, which links the island of Manhattan to Long Island, was opened in 1883, and quickly became an iconic feature of the New York skyline. Not only was the bridge an ambitious engineering project which showed that America's technological and industrial capabilities had grown to equal those of its European competitors; the bridge was also a symbol of the fast-developing nation's ideals and aspirations. At the bridge's opening, Abram S. Hewitt, a congressman and industrialist, celebrated the new structure as a sign of man's ability to subdue nature. He said: 'It stands before us today as the sum and epitome of human knowledge.' Brooklyn Bridge has featured prominently in American art, literature and film, from its opening to the twenty-first century.

Part Four: Using sources

Plagiarism exercise

Robert MacDougall (2007) notes that American society in the second half of the nineteenth century was troubled by the concept of action at a distance made possible by new technologies, including the telephone and the telegraph and the railroad. As MacDougall explains, in the decades after the Civil War, American railroads 'linked the corners of the continent with thousands of miles of track' (p.216). Starting in 1861, telegraph companies also begain to span the nation, providing 'instantaneous communication from coast to coast'. He also notes that after 1876, the telephone quickly eclipsed the telegraph, creating new national networks of communication.

Your answer should read something like this. Note that the author of the article is mentioned before his ideas are used. Also, direct quotes from the text are put in quotation marks and are given page numbers. This version makes the source of its information clear, and sounds more authoritative.

Referencing exercise

1 Author–date system reference list

Brown, J. (1995) *Charles Darwin: Voyaging.* London: Jonathan Cape.

Horz, H. (1979) 'Philosophical Concepts of Space and Time'. *In* A. P. French, *Einstein: A Centenary Volume*. London: Heinemann, pp.229–41.

Marsden, B. and Smith, C. (2005) *Engineering Empires – A Cultural History of Technology in Nineteenth-Century Britain*. London: Palgrave.

Mandell, L. (2007) 'Imaging Interiority: Photography, Psychology, and Lyric Poetry'. *Victorian Studies,* 49 (2), pp.218–28.

Weber, A. S. ed. (2000) *19th Century Science: An Anthology.* Peterborough, Ontario: Broadview Press.

Zola, E. (1996) *La Bête Humaine* (R. Pearson. Trans). Oxford: Oxford University Press (original work published 1890).

2 MHRA style bibliography

Brown, Janet, *Charles Darwin: Voyaging* (London: Jonathan Cape, 1995)

Horz, Herbert, 'Philosophical Concepts of Space and Time', *Einstein a Centenary Volume,* ed. by A. P. French (London: Heinemann, 1979), 229–41

Marsden, Ben and Crosbie Smith, *Engineering Empires: A Cultural History of Technology in Nineteenth-Century Britain* (London: Palgrave, 2005)

Mandell, Laura, 'Imaging Interiority: Photography, Psychology, and Lyric Poetry', *Victorian Studies,* 49 (2), (2007) 218–28

Weber, A. S. (ed.), *19th Century Science: An Anthology* (Peterborough, Ontario: Broadview Press, 2000)

Zola, Emile, *La Bête Humaine* (1890), trans. by Roger Pearson, (Oxford: Oxford University Press, 1996)

There are many study guides available on the subject of writing skills, both in print and online. The following is a list of books and online sources consulted during the preparation of this book and recommended as further reading. This list is set out in MHRA bibliography style.

Print resources

Barass, Robert, *Scientists Must Write: A Guide to Better Writing for Scientists, Engineers and Students* (London: Routledge, 2002)

British Standards Institute, *BS5605:1990 Recommendations for Citing and Referencing Published Material*, 2nd ed. (London: British Standards Institution, 1990)

Burchfield, R. W., ed., *Fowler's Modern English Usage*, 3rd ed. (Oxford: Oxford University Press, 1998)

Clancy, John and Brigit Ballard, *How to Write Essays: A Practical Guide for Students* (Harlow: Longman, 1998)

Cottrell, Stella, *Critical Thinking Skills: Developing Effective Analysis and Argument* (London: Palgrave, 2005)

Gee, Robyn, and Carol Watson, *Usborne Guide to Better English: Grammar, Spelling and Punctuation* (London: Usborne, 2004)

Greetham, Bryan, *How to Write Better Essays* (London: Palgrave, 1999)

Hennesey, Brendan, *Writing an Essay* (Oxford: How to Books, 2002)

Lindsay, David, *A Guide to Scientific Writing: Manual for Students and Research Workers*, 2nd ed. (London: Longman, 1996)

Mounsey, Chris, *Essays and Dissertations* (Oxford: Oxford University Press, 2002)

Neville, Colin, *The Complete Guide to Referencing and Avoiding Plagiarism* (Maidenhead: Open University Press, 2007)

Partridge, Eric, *Usage and Abusage: A Guide to Good English* (Harmondsworth: Penguin, 1999)

Peck, John and Martin Coyle, *Practical Criticism: How to Write a Critical Appreciation* (Houndmills: Palgrave, 1985)

Peck, John, and Martin Coyle, *The Student's Guide to Writing: Grammar, Spelling and Punctuation* (Houndmills: Palgrave, 1999)

Price, Glanville, *MHRA Style Book,* 6th ed. (London: Modern Humanities Research Association, 2002)

Phythian, B. A. and Albert Rowe, *Teach Yourself Correct English* (London: Hodder, 2003)

Ritter, R. M., (ed)., *The Oxford Dictionary for Writers and Editors*, 2nd ed. (Oxford: Oxford University Press, 2000)

Simpson, Ron, *Teach Yourself English Grammar* (London: Hodder, 2003)

Sinclair, Christine, *Grammar: A Friendly Approach* (Maidenhead: Open University Press, 2007)

Stott, Rebecca and Rick Rylance, *Making Your Case: A Practical Guide to Essay Writing* (London: Longman, 2000)

Strunk, William and E. B. White, *The Elements of Style* (London: Longman, 1999)

Truss, Lynne, *Eats, Shoots and Leaves: The Zero-Tolerance Approach to Punctuation* (London: Profile Books, 2003)

Walmsley, Bernice, *Teach Yourself Good Study Skills* (London: Hodder, 2006)

Online resources

British Standards Institute, BS5605:1990 *Recommendations for Citing and Referencing Published Material.* http://www.bsonline.bsi-global.com/server/index.jsp

Clark, Robert, *The English Style Book: A Guide to the Writing of Scholarly English.* http://www.litencyc.com/stylebook/stylebook.php

Kennedy, David, *Essay Writing a Guide for Undergraduates*. http://www.rlf.org.uk/fellowshipscheme/writing/index.cfm

MHRA Style Guide Online. http://www.mhra.org.uk/ Publications/Books/StyleGuide/

Holland, M., 2005, *Citing References* (July 2005). http://www.bournemouth.ac.uk/academicsupport/document s/Library/Citing_References.pdf

University of Hull Study Advice Service, *Academic Writing and Study Skills*. http://www.hull.ac.uk/studyavice/serv_info/ reso_acad.htm

Reference list

The following is a list of the works referred to or used as examples within the text of the book. This list is set out in author–date/Harvard style.

Austen, J. (1996) *Pride and Prejudice*. London: Penguin (originally published 1813).

Barthes, Roland (1977) 'The Death of the Author.' In *Image-Music-Text*. (S. Heath. Trans) Glasgow: Collins.

Beach, W. (1954) *The Method of Henry James*. Philadelphia, Albert Saifer.

Bradbury, N. (1979) *Henry James, The Later Novels*. Oxford: Oxford University Press.

Dickens, C. (1843) *A Christmas Carol. In* S. Ledger, ed. (1999) *The Christmas Books*. London: Everyman.

Dickens, C. (1994) *Great Expectations*. London: Everyman (originally published 1861).

Frost, R. (2001) *The Poetry of Robert Frost*. Ed. E. C. Lathem. London: Cape (originally published 1971).

Hopkins, G. M. (1979) *The Major Poems*. Ed. W. Davies. London: Dent.

Hutchison, H. (2006) *Seeing and Believing: Henry James and the Spiritual World*. New York: Palgrave.

Jones, E. (1910) 'The Oedipus-Complex as An Explanation of Hamlet's Mystery: A Study in Motive'. *American Journal of Psychology*, 21, pp. 72–113.

Kaplan, J. (2006) *When the Astors Owned New York: Blue Bloods and Grand Hotels in a Gilded Age.* New York: Viking.

Keegan, P. ed. (2000) *The Penguin Book of English Verse.* London: Penguin.

Leavis, F. R. (1948) *The Great Tradition.* London: Chatto and Windus.

Matthiessen, F. O. (1944) *Henry James: The Major Phase.* Oxford: Oxford University Press.

Shakespeare, W. (1968) *Hamlet.* In *The Complete Works of Shakespeare.* Vol. II. New York: Nelson Doubleday.

Truss, L. (2003) *Eats, Shoots and Leaves: The Zero Tolerance Approach to Punctuation.* London: Profile Books.

teach yourself ®

From Advanced Sudoku to Zulu, you'll find everything you need in the **teach yourself** range, in books, on CD and on DVD.

Visit **www.teachyourself.co.uk** for more details.

Advanced Sudoku and Kakuro
Afrikaans
Alexander Technique
Algebra
Ancient Greek
Applied Psychology
Arabic
Aromatherapy
Art History
Astrology
Astronomy
AutoCAD 2004
AutoCAD 2007
Ayurveda
Baby Massage and Yoga
Baby Signing
Baby Sleep
Bach Flower Remedies
Backgammon
Ballroom Dancing
Basic Accounting
Basic Computer Skills
Basic Mathematics
Beauty
Beekeeping
Beginner's Arabic Script
Beginner's Chinese Script
Beginner's Dutch

Beginner's French
Beginner's German
Beginner's Greek
Beginner's Greek Script
Beginner's Hindi
Beginner's Italian
Beginner's Japanese
Beginner's Japanese Script
Beginner's Latin
Beginner's Mandarin Chinese
Beginner's Portuguese
Beginner's Russian
Beginner's Russian Script
Beginner's Spanish
Beginner's Turkish
Beginner's Urdu Script
Bengali
Better Bridge
Better Chess
Better Driving
Better Handwriting
Biblical Hebrew
Biology
Birdwatching
Blogging
Body Language
Book Keeping
Brazilian Portuguese

Bridge
British Empire, The
British Monarchy from Henry
   VIII, The
Buddhism
Bulgarian
Business Chinese
Business French
Business Japanese
Business Plans
Business Spanish
Business Studies
Buying a Home in France
Buying a Home in Italy
Buying a Home in Portugal
Buying a Home in Spain
C++
Calculus
Calligraphy
Cantonese
Car Buying and Maintenance
Card Games
Catalan
Chess
Chi Kung
Chinese Medicine
Christianity
Classical Music
Coaching
Cold War, The
Collecting
Computing for the Over 50s
Consulting
Copywriting
Correct English
Counselling
Creative Writing
Cricket
Croatian
Crystal Healing
CVs
Czech
Danish
Decluttering
Desktop Publishing
Detox

Digital Home Movie Making
Digital Photography
Dog Training
Drawing
Dream Interpretation
Dutch
Dutch Conversation
Dutch Dictionary
Dutch Grammar
Eastern Philosophy
Electronics
English as a Foreign Language
English for International
   Business
English Grammar
English Grammar as a Foreign
   Language
English Vocabulary
Entrepreneurship
Estonian
Ethics
Excel 2003
Feng Shui
Film Making
Film Studies
Finance for Non-Financial
   Managers
Finnish
First World War, The
Fitness
Flash 8
Flash MX
Flexible Working
Flirting
Flower Arranging
Franchising
French
French Conversation
French Dictionary
French Grammar
French Phrasebook
French Starter Kit
French Verbs
French Vocabulary
Freud
Gaelic

Gardening
Genetics
Geology
German
German Conversation
German Grammar
German Phrasebook
German Verbs
German Vocabulary
Globalization
Go
Golf
Good Study Skills
Great Sex
Greek
Greek Conversation
Greek Phrasebook
Growing Your Business
Guitar
Gulf Arabic
Hand Reflexology
Hausa
Herbal Medicine
Hieroglyphics
Hindi
Hindi Conversation
Hinduism
History of Ireland, The
Home PC Maintenance and
  Networking
How to DJ
How to Run a Marathon
How to Win at Casino Games
How to Win at Horse Racing
How to Win at Online Gambling
How to Win at Poker
How to Write a Blockbuster
Human Anatomy & Physiology
Hungarian
Icelandic
Improve Your French
Improve Your German
Improve Your Italian
Improve Your Spanish
Improving Your Employability

Indian Head Massage
Indonesian
Instant French
Instant German
Instant Greek
Instant Italian
Instant Japanese
Instant Portuguese
Instant Russian
Instant Spanish
Internet, The
Irish
Irish Conversation
Irish Grammar
Islam
Italian
Italian Conversation
Italian Grammar
Italian Phrasebook
Italian Starter Kit
Italian Verbs
Italian Vocabulary
Japanese
Japanese Conversation
Java
JavaScript
Jazz
Jewellery Making
Judaism
Jung
Kama Sutra, The
Keeping Aquarium Fish
Keeping Pigs
Keeping Poultry
Keeping a Rabbit
Knitting
Korean
Latin
Latin American Spanish
Latin Dictionary
Latin Grammar
Latvian
Letter Writing Skills
Life at 50: For Men
Life at 50: For Women

Life Coaching
Linguistics
LINUX
Lithuanian
Magic
Mahjong
Malay
Managing Stress
Managing Your Own Career
Mandarin Chinese
Mandarin Chinese Conversation
Marketing
Marx
Massage
Mathematics
Meditation
Middle East Since 1945, The
Modern China
Modern Hebrew
Modern Persian
Mosaics
Music Theory
Mussolini's Italy
Nazi Germany
Negotiating
Nepali
New Testament Greek
NLP
Norwegian
Norwegian Conversation
Old English
One-Day French
One-Day French – the DVD
One-Day German
One-Day Greek
One-Day Italian
One-Day Portuguese
One-Day Spanish
One-Day Spanish – the DVD
Origami
Owning a Cat
Owning a Horse
Panjabi
PC Networking for Small
  Businesses

Personal Safety and Self
  Defence
Philosophy
Philosophy of Mind
Philosophy of Religion
Photography
Photoshop
PHP with MySQL
Physics
Piano
Pilates
Planning Your Wedding
Polish
Polish Conversation
Politics
Portuguese
Portuguese Conversation
Portuguese Grammar
Portuguese Phrasebook
Postmodernism
Pottery
PowerPoint 2003
PR
Project Management
Psychology
Quick Fix French Grammar
Quick Fix German Grammar
Quick Fix Italian Grammar
Quick Fix Spanish Grammar
Quick Fix: Access 2002
Quick Fix: Excel 2000
Quick Fix: Excel 2002
Quick Fix: HTML
Quick Fix: Windows XP
Quick Fix: Word
Quilting
Recruitment
Reflexology
Reiki
Relaxation
Retaining Staff
Romanian
Running Your Own Business
Russian
Russian Conversation

Russian Grammar
Sage Line 50
Sanskrit
Screenwriting
Second World War, The
Serbian
Setting Up a Small Business
Shorthand Pitman 2000
Sikhism
Singing
Slovene
Small Business Accounting
Small Business Health Check
Songwriting
Spanish
Spanish Conversation
Spanish Dictionary
Spanish Grammar
Spanish Phrasebook
Spanish Starter Kit
Spanish Verbs
Spanish Vocabulary
Speaking On Special Occasions
Speed Reading
Stalin's Russia
Stand Up Comedy
Statistics
Stop Smoking
Sudoku
Swahili
Swahili Dictionary
Swedish
Swedish Conversation
Tagalog
Tai Chi
Tantric Sex
Tap Dancing
Teaching English as a Foreign
    Language
Teams & Team Working
Thai
Theatre
Time Management
Tracing Your Family History
Training

Travel Writing
Trigonometry
Turkish
Turkish Conversation
Twentieth Century USA
Typing
Ukrainian
Understanding Tax for Small
    Businesses
Understanding Terrorism
Urdu
Vietnamese
Visual Basic
Volcanoes
Watercolour Painting
Weight Control through Diet &
    Exercise
Welsh
Welsh Dictionary
Welsh Grammar
Wills & Probate
Windows XP
Wine Tasting
Winning at Job Interviews
Word 2003
World Cultures: China
World Cultures: England
World Cultures: Germany
World Cultures: Italy
World Cultures: Japan
World Cultures: Portugal
World Cultures: Russia
World Cultures: Spain
World Cultures: Wales
World Faiths
Writing Crime Fiction
Writing for Children
Writing for Magazines
Writing a Novel
Writing Poetry
Xhosa
Yiddish
Yoga
Zen
Zulu

teach
yourself

good study skills
bernice walmsley

- Are you a new or out-of-practice learner?
- Do you want tips for reading, reviewing – and passing?
- Do you need help writing projects?

Whether you have just started an evening or training course or even driving lessons, **Good Study Skills** will help you study effectively. From speed reading to writing essays and presentations, it is full of practical techniques, step-by-step instructions and review tests to practice your new skills. With help for those baffled by technology and ample supporting resources, it is ideal for any new or returning learner.

Bernice Walmsley is a full-time writer specializing in educational and business learning.

| teach yourself | **correct english** |
| | b. a. phythian & albert rowe |

- Do you need help with writing English?
- Do you want a guide to the rules of grammar, punctuation and spelling?
- Do you worry that you sometimes make mistakes?

Correct English is a practical guide and reference book which will help you to improve your command of both spoken and written English, whether you are preparing for an English examination or simply want to improve your language skills. Learn how to avoid the commonest mistakes and pitfalls and increase your confidence to write letters, summaries, reports and essays.

B. A. Phythian's classic has been extensively simplified and updated by **Albert Rowe**, an experienced English teacher of many years.

| teach yourself | **managing stress** |
| | terry looker & olga gregson |

- Do you want to understand the theory behind managing stress?
- Do you want to identify the sources of stress in your life?
- Are you looking for your own stress management plan?

Managing Stress is a step-by-step guide to dealing with stress, leading to a healthier, more relaxed and enjoyable way of life. The questionnaire to assess your stress levels will enable you to identify the signs, symptoms and sources of stress. You will understand what is happening to you mentally and physically and you will learn coping strategies to bring balance to your life.

Professor Terry Looker and **Dr Olga Gregson** are Fellows of the International Stress Management Association. They lecture at the Manchester Metropolitan University and worldwide and present stress management programmes for industry and the professions.

teach
yourself

writing a novel
nigel watts

- Do you want to turn your ideas into a novel?
- Do you need to overcome writer's block?
- Are you looking for advice on getting published?

Writing a Novel takes you through the whole process of writing a novel, from the germ of an idea, through developing plot, character and theme, to preparing it for publication. This fascinating analysis will appeal to both new and experienced authors alike.

Nigel Watts, PhD in Creative and Critical Writing, taught from 1989, the year in which he published his first award-winning novel, *The Life Game*. He went on to publish four further novels for adults, two children's stories and an anthology of spiritual poetry.